P R A Y I N G

WITH POWER

WHEN ANYONE ASKS ME WHICH OF MY BOOKS ABOUT prayer best gives the whole picture, this is the one!

C. Peter Wagner

PRAYING WITH POWER

Praying with Power is profound and stimulating! This is Peter Wagner's best overall book on prayer—a dynamic summary of what Wagner has learned about prayer during the last decade. You will want to buy copies for your friends as well as for yourself.

DAVID YONGGI CHO
SENIOR PASTOR, YOIDO FULL GOSPEL CHURCH
SEOUL, SOUTH KOREA

Praying with Power is Peter Wagner's best book yet. A great tool for personal prayer development, this anointed book brings an understanding into the work of prayer that will move you beyond traditional forms of prayer and into truly effective intercession.

ROBERTS LIARDON
PASTOR, EMBASSY CHRISTIAN CENTER
IRVINE, CALIFORNIA

C. PETER WAGNER

PRAYING WITH POWER

HOW TO PRAY EFFECTIVELY AND HEAR CLEARLY FROM GOD

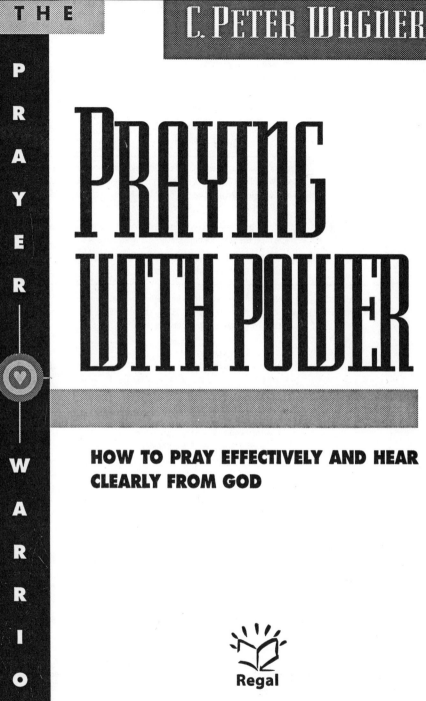

Regal

A Division of Gospel Light
Ventura, California, U.S.A.

THE PRAYER WARRIOR SERIES

Published by Regal Books
A Division of Gospel Light
Ventura, California, U.S.A.
Printed in U.S.A.

Regal Books is a ministry of Gospel Light, an evangelical Christian publisher dedicated to serving the local church. We believe God's vision for Gospel Light is to provide church leaders with biblical, user-friendly materials that will help them evangelize, disciple and minister to children, youth and families.

It is our prayer that this Regal book will help you discover biblical truth for your own life and help you meet the needs of others. May God richly bless you.

For a free catalog of resources from Regal Books/Gospel Light please contact your Christian supplier or call 1-800-4-GOSPEL.

All Scripture quotations, unless otherwise indicated, are taken from the
New King James Version. Copyright © 1979, 1980, 1982 by Thomas Nelson, Inc. Publishers.
Used by permission. All rights reserved.

Other version used is:
CEV—Contemporary English Version. The Promise™ copyright © 1995, Thomas Nelson, Inc.

© Copyright 1997 by C. Peter Wagner
All rights reserved.

Cover Design by Barbara LeVan Fisher
Interior Design by Britt Rocchio
Edited by Virginia Woodard

Library of Congress Cataloging-in-Publication Data
Wagner, C. Peter.
    Praying with Power / C. Peter Wagner.
        p. cm. — (The Prayer warrior series)
    Includes bibliographical references and index.
    ISBN 0-8307-1919-9 (trade paper)
    1. Prayer—Christianity. I. Title. II. Series.
    BV210.2.W24 1997   97-10999
    248.3'2—dc21   CIP

2 3 4 5 6 7 8 9 10 11 12 13 14 15 / 04 03 02 01 00 99 98

Rights for publishing this book in other languages are contracted by Gospel Literature International (GLINT). GLINT also provides technical help for the adaptation, translation and publishing of Bible study resources and books in scores of languages worldwide. For further information, contact GLINT, P.O. Box 4060, Ontario, CA 91761-1003, U.S.A., or the publisher

Contents

Introduction

TEN YEARS AGO I NEVER THOUGHT I WOULD WRITE AN *article* about prayer, to say nothing of a whole book. How things change!

The book you have in your hand is the sixth volume in *The Prayer Warrior Series,* containing a cumulative total of more than 1,500 pages. Back in 1987, God gave me the assignment of researching, writing and teaching about how prayer relates to advancing the kingdom of God through missions, church planting and church growth. I knew so little about prayer at the time that I thought I was getting a boring assignment. I also wondered why God would choose to do such a thing to me at this stage of life. I now know, however, that God did not plan to bore me, but rather to bless me.

These past 10 years have proven to be by far the most exciting ones out of more than 40 years of ordained ministry!

CAN PRAYER BE "ASSUMED"?

I became so enthusiastic about my involvement in the world-wide prayer movement that some of my friends thought I had abandoned my calling as a professor of church growth. That was because my colleagues and I in the field of church growth had not previously paid much attention to spiritual factors such as prayer. We believed in prayer all right, but we had *assumed* that prayer would always be there, and that not much could be said about it anyhow. When I discovered that such was far from the truth, I was misunderstood for a time by some of my friends.

Those days are past, though, thank the Lord. Books, tapes and conferences about prayer are difficult to keep track of because they are multiplying almost too rapidly. I now have 9 shelves of books about prayer in my personal library, soon to be 10.

As I travel across the country and into many other parts of the world, people frequently ask me which one of my prayer books I would recommend they read. This question reflects the fact that many people can think in terms of only one book at a time. Some do not have a personal budget large enough to purchase many books. Others may be able to read, but they are not habitual book readers. Certain people feel a considerable sense of accomplishment if they read just one or two books during the period of a year.

To be honest, I have not had a ready answer for that question about recommending books in the past. In the rare instances when I have time, I talk with the people long enough to attempt to discern their needs and then I try to name the book that will help them the most. My problem is that each one of the first five books of *The Prayer Warrior Series* is specialized and targeted toward a certain kind of prayer to meet a certain set of needs.

WHEN YOU MUST CHOOSE JUST ONE

From now on, I will tell those who think they can handle only one of my books about prayer to read this one—*Praying with Power.* True, it is the last one, but I have written it as an introduction to the whole series. In this book, I have picked up the major threads of the other five books and tried to put them all together. This is the overview of all the subjects I have written about, and those who are interested can move from here to obtain the other books and then delve deeper into any of the themes that especially interest them.

You will find a couple of emphases in this book that are not included in the others, namely identificational repentance (chapter 5) and prophetic prayer acts (chapter 10). You will also find a certain amount of overlap with the other books, but I tried to keep that to a minimum. I did not copy anything directly from the other five books in this one, and it does not contain as much overlap as we find, for example, in the four Gospels. Nevertheless, I am the same author and I thought it necessary to repeat some of the things I consider among the most important. I like to look at it as "creative redundancy."

I have mentioned the other books from time to time in this one. This is not intended to be a promotional stunt to get people to buy the other books. It is, rather, my attempt to provide readers with a road map of sorts for moving in a variety of directions as the Lord leads. I have listed further resources at the end of each chapter for readers who wish to read more about the subject.

This book is also an update. I have learned a great deal since I wrote my first book about prayer five years ago, and I am excited about sharing many of the newer things God has been showing us. The Bible says there is nothing new under the sun. This is true, but it is equally true that I as an individual have been discovering things I never knew before, and the same would be said by those representing many substantial segments of the Body of Christ.

Christian people are praying and talking about prayer more than at any time in memory. Pastors are elevating prayer toward the top of their agendas for the local church.

Seminaries and Bible schools are teaching courses about prayer that they have never taught before. Denominations and mission agencies are adding prayer leaders to their top-level staffs. New independent prayer ministries are multiplying on every continent.

This is the time for you to be informed, and for you to become involved. My prayer is that this book, *Praying with Power,* will be used by the Lord to bring thousands and thousands into the mainstream of the worldwide prayer movement, and that His name will be exalted among the nations as it never has before!

C. Peter Wagner
Colorado Springs, Colorado

Prayer Can Be Powerful (Or Otherwise)

THE NAME OF THE CHURCH IS THE PRAYER CAVE. This might seem like an odd name to the ears of most American believers. All across Kenya, however, the most prominent nation of East Africa, creativity reigns in assigning church names. When he founded the church in the small city of Kiambu not long ago, prayer had played such a vital role for Pastor Thomas Muthee that calling it "The Prayer Cave" was a natural.

No other church I am aware of better exemplifies what this book is all about—praying with power. I think it is important for us to understand that prayer is not some ethereal exercise that has little measurable effect on the real world in which we live. I know of no better way to begin to understand how powerful prayer can be than to explore a concrete example such as The Prayer Cave in Kiambu, Kenya.

Prayer Truly Works

A central thesis underlying all my writings about prayer is that prayer works. Not all prayer works, but *effective* prayer does. *Powerful* prayer works. I have emphasized those adjectives to highlight what many of us already know in our hearts, but sometimes hesitate to admit—not all prayer is equal. Just as some prayer is effective, so some is ineffective, and some is in between. Just as some prayer is powerful, so, unfortunately, some is equally impotent. I am enough of a born pragmatist to have virtually no incentive to write a series of books about prayer in general. My interest is almost exclusively in *powerful* prayer, not in the other kinds.

The essence of prayer is a personal relationship between a believer and God. Some call it "intimacy with the Father." This is true, and it is important. For this reason it would not be correct to say that any believing prayer is *bad* per se. I would not want to make a distinction between *good* prayer and *bad* prayer, for example. Some prayer, however, we must admit, can be misguided and therefore lack the power it could have. James says, "You ask and do not receive, because you ask amiss" (Jas. 4:3). Wrong motives can weaken prayer, as can sin in our lives and many other things I will mention from time to time as we move on.

The distinction I am making is, more accurately, between *good* prayer and *better* prayer. My wife, Doris, likes to say, "No prayer is wasted." All good prayer can be seen as a step in the right direction, but some of those steps may be smaller than they need to be. If you are reading this book, the odds are high that you have a burning desire in your heart to pray more powerfully than you ordinarily have been doing. You may be on a relatively low level right now, but you do not want to stay there. You may be on a high level of prayer power, but you know that there are higher levels yet, and that is where you want to be.

MEASURING THE POWER OF PRAYER

How will you know when you reach a higher level of prayer? One way is to see an increase in concrete, measurable answers to your prayers. That is why I like to assert that prayer works. James does not say, "the prayer of a righteous man avails much." He seems to go out of his way to say that "the *effective, fervent* prayer of a righteous [person] avails much" (5:16, emphasis added). If he had left it at that point, the statement would certainly have been true, although somewhat vague. To avoid this, James immediately goes on to make it more concrete. He uses Elijah, a human being just like us, as his example. Elijah prayed that it would not rain, and it did not. Then he prayed that it would rain, and it did. Elijah's prayers worked!

I wish all my prayers would be like Elijah's. I must confess, however, that I have not arrived at Elijah's level—*yet*. I am not even at the level of many of my closest friends—*yet*. One thing I do know is that I am on a higher level than I was last year, and that next year I intend, with God's help, to be higher than I am now. I may never reach Elijah's level, but it is not because such a thing is impossible.

In the passage I am citing, James takes pains to point out that "Elijah was a man with a nature like ours" (v. 17). It is certainly possible that God could use you and that He could use me the way He used Elijah. Why not? That is exactly what I desire. I want my prayers to be more effective in the future than they have been in the past.

This book, I have no doubt, will help your prayers become more powerful than they have been in the past. Just feeling the pulse of a dynamic church such as The Prayer Cave will fill you with renewed faith and hope for effective prayer in your personal life, in the lives of your family, in your church and in your community. I think you will agree with me that Pastor Thomas Muthee is fairly close to the Elijah level.

THE KENYA PRAYER CAVE

Pastor Thomas Muthee is a valued personal friend. He is my East African director of the International Spiritual Warfare Network and one of 13 distinguished members of the World Prayer Center International Board. He is a clear thinker, articulate, wise and respected by his peers in Africa and other parts of the world. I say this, not to inflate my friend Thomas, but simply to assure the readers that we are not talking about some obscure flake, but about a church leader of good reputation and high integrity.

I am deeply grateful to my colleague, George Otis Jr. of The Sentinel Group, for introducing me to Pastor Thomas Muthee and for interviewing him to collect details of this remarkable story. The following story is paraphrased from George Otis Jr.'s forthcoming book, *The Twilight of the Labyrinth* (Chosen Books).

Thomas Muthee would be commonly identified as a megachurch pastor. The Prayer Cave church is growing rapidly and, at this writing, approaching 4,000 members, or 5 percent of Kiambu's population of 80,000. Almost all the members are new converts because very few residents of Kiambu were Christians when Thomas arrived. How did this church grow so vigorously, and how did it come to have such a measurable influence on the whole city?

Without any hesitation whatsoever, Thomas Muthee would say that it happened through *powerful prayer.*

Thomas and his wife had returned to Kenya from a time in Scotland in the late 1980s. He was ministering as an itinerant evangelist and his wife was teaching school. While in prayer one day in 1988, he heard the Lord say to him, "I want you to plant a church in Kiambu." Hearing from the Lord in prayer was not a new experience for Thomas, although it would be for many Christians whom I know. This is such a vital component of powerful prayer that I have dedicated the entire next chapter to the subject of two-way prayer.

After spending a good deal more time with the Lord and testing the word with his wife and others—always a good safeguard—Thomas was certain this was indeed the command of God for a new career and for a new place of residence. There was no question in his mind that he had to obey. Thomas, however, did not look forward to the assignment with one bit of pleasure.

A Murder Capital and a Preacher's Graveyard

Kiambu? Only a few miles distant from the beautiful capital city of Nairobi, Kiambu had gained a national reputation for having the worst crime, violence, drunkenness, immorality, thievery and human degradation. Public disorder was the rule and loud rock music was blaring from speakers in front of barrooms throughout the nights. It was the murder capital of Kenya, registering up to eight killings in a given month. The economy of the city was so bad that government officials reportedly paid bribes to their superiors so as not to be assigned to Kiambu.

A cloud of mystery also hung over the city. Everyone there knew that in one certain place many and often unexplainable automobile accidents regularly occurred. It was considered a good month when as few as three fatalities were reported as a result of traffic accidents. Stranger still was the fact that no matter how mangled the bodies of the accident victims were, to all intents and purposes, no bleeding occurred—ever! At times, some reported hearing screeching tires and crashing metal, but when they ran to the site, no cars could be seen at all!

Although he had never visited Kiambu, Thomas knew its

reputation well and he did not like the city, much less the prospects of making his home there. Add to that the fact that, although he had been in Christian ministry for years, he had never contemplated planting a new church. He believed he had the gift of evangelist, and he was using it successfully as he traveled around the nation.

Even if he had intended to plant a church, Kiambu would have been Muthee's last choice as a likely site because the city had also gained the reputation as a preacher's graveyard. Pastor after pastor tried to plant a church there and soon left defeated and discouraged. The Pentecostal/charismatic kind of churches, which were growing vigorously in other parts of Kenya, could not seem to grow either in Kiambu. The largest, pastored by a wonderful, dedicated man of God, had grown to less than 60 members after 15 years of faithful ministry! Another, also 15 years old, had 40 members, and another only 30.

Six Months of Prayer and Fasting

The assignment was clear; but how to implement it? If Thomas had taken my course at Fuller in church planting, he might have conducted demographic surveys, feasibility studies, public opinion polls and cost analyses studies. Not that any of these are bad—I continue to recommend them highly to the best of intelligent church planters. God, however, gave Thomas a different strategy few church planters have used, but in this case it was probably the one way a city as engulfed by spiritual darkness as Kiambu could be penetrated to any significant degree by the gospel.

By mentioning this, I do not want to leave the impression that I am suggesting Thomas Muthee's method should be *substituted* for tried-and-true church growth and church-planting principles. I definitely *do*, however, want to leave the impression that church planters of any stripe would do well to take a close look at what Thomas did, discern the spiritual principles behind his activities and, although they decide not to copy his method, at least consider employing the principles.

God's plan for Thomas and his wife was for them to pray and fast for six months, which they faithfully did. Thomas did not so much as visit Kiambu, only 10 miles from his home, during that time period. They practiced a variety of fasts during those months, sometimes fasting a meal or two, sometimes for extended periods, drinking juice or water only, as well as some absolute fasts when they consumed no food or drink.

I personally heard Thomas describe this season of waiting on the Lord. He saw it as proactive spiritual warfare. He said, "If we are going to win the battle for Kiambu, we must win it in the air. The ground troops must not invade the territory of the enemy without first achieving victory in the invisible world. I would not want to step my foot into Kiambu until the spiritual forces of darkness over the city have lost their grip."

Thomas was no stranger to the devices of Satan. He was an experienced intercessor and in his evangelistic work he had confronted the enemy in power encounters on a variety of levels. He had learned that the devil assigns certain specific demons over towns, cities and nations, as well as families. He said, "Over this extended time of prayer and fasting, I wanted to know exactly what was keeping Kiambu so politically, socially, economically and spiritually oppressed."

The term many of us are using for the quest that was engaging Thomas Muthee at the time is "spiritual mapping." The major purpose of spiritual mapping is to target our prayers as accurately as possible. This is so important that I have written a whole chapter about the subject (chapter 4). So I will not go into much detail here except to say that as Thomas prayed, he found himself asking more and more for the exact identity of the major principality over the city. As I often say, it is not *necessary* to know the name of the chief spirit to pray effectively for a city such as Kiambu, but if God chooses to reveal the name, it is an *advantage*. In this case, Thomas believed he should ask specifically for the name.

The Power over the City: Witchcraft

God answered, this time through a vision. In the vision, Thomas clearly saw the principality over Kiambu, and its name was "Witchcraft." He also saw many other demons around Witchcraft and under its command. From that point onward, the prayers of Thomas and his wife were much more specifically targeted, and they sensed in the Spirit that considerable damage was being done in the invisible world to the dark angels that had enjoyed such a free reign over Kiambu for generations.

The name they received was a *functional* name—a spirit of witchcraft. That demon might well have also had a *proper* name, similar to some we read about in the Bible such as "Wormwood" or "Abaddon" or "Beelzebub," but in this instance Thomas apparently did not need to know what it was. If he needed it, God would undoubtedly have revealed it to him. At the same time, the vision was so clear that Thomas assigned the proper name, "Witchcraft," to the spirit who was controlling that activity and thereby influencing much of what was happening in the city.

At the end of the six months of prayer and fasting, Thomas felt peace in his heart and mind. He sensed that the major phase of the ministry to reach Kiambu with the gospel had been completed. He saw in the Spirit that the spiritual atmosphere over Kiambu had been sufficiently cleared through powerful prayer and that the forces of darkness over the city were losing their stranglehold on the city and were now in disarray. It was time for the ground forces to move into enemy territory.

Invasion: By an Army of Two!

The ground forces consisted of only two people—Thomas and his wife. When they moved there, though, they discovered that the way had been prepared so well that they were the first Christian ministers allowed to use the Kiambu municipal hall to preach the gospel.

Their strategy was to win people through public evangelistic meetings, so Thomas, drawing on his extensive experience as an evangelist, began the meetings in January 1989. One of

---

"What is gained by prayer must be maintained by prayer!"

---

the first things he did was to borrow some used tires from a local mechanic, because Thomas is very short. He piled them up, fashioned a platform, preached the Word and saw eight people saved the first night!

The evangelistic harvest continued, and the new church met in the municipal hall for more than a year. Thomas became more and more dissatisfied, though, because they could not pray on site enough. They had use of the building on Sundays and on Wednesday nights only. Thomas's vision was that his church facility should be used for prayer 24 hours a day, every day. He knew well what I have heard many intercessors say, "What is gained by prayer must be maintained by prayer!" He was convinced that if his new church was to continue to grow and ultimately have an influence on the whole city of Kiambu, prayer had to be the most prominent ongoing component of his philosophy of ministry.

Soon they were able to move out of the municipal hall, but

only into the basement of another building. It might have been rather dark and dingy, but from the day they moved in, the 24-hour prayer has never stopped! Going into the basement felt something like going into a cave, so people naturally began referring to it as The Prayer Cave, and the name stuck. The church, as might be expected, has a more official name (Word of Faith Church), but it is known far and wide only as The Kiambu Prayer Cave, although it no longer meets in the basement.

The Spiritual Counterattack

The way I am narrating this case study might sound as if the first couple of years of The Prayer Cave were a piece of cake—no problems; no heartaches; no setbacks. On the contrary, the spiritual counterattack was fierce. Thomas soon discovered that the human being whom the principality over the city, Witchcraft, was using the most was a notorious sorcerer named "Momma Jane." She did her witchcraft and fortune-telling in a place she had perversely named "Emmanuel Clinic." She was considered by many as the most powerful person in the city, and both politicians and businesspeople frequented Emmanuel Clinic to have their fortunes told and to receive Momma Jane's blessing.

One more thing—the Emmanuel Clinic happened to be located near an open market and precisely at that part of the city where the mysterious fatal traffic accidents had been occurring month after month!

Every Saturday night Momma Jane went to Muthee's church site, performed magic and cast her spells and curses. She let it be known to the city officials that she could not help them with her fortune-telling as much as she used to because this new church seemed to be "cutting her lines of communication." Consequently, one of the outcomes was that not only the city authorities, but also the pastors of other Christian churches were attacking the ministry of The Prayer Cave. That part of it was no fun!

Thomas Muthee and the church members, praying 24 hours a day, did what they could to counteract the demonic attacks against the church. Some Christian leaders seem to think that Christians are immune to Satan's attacks. They trivialize the devil by calling him a "toothless lion." Such an attitude of denial only plays into Satan's hands and gives him free rein to continue his plans to kill, steal and destroy. Such was not the case with the members of The Prayer Cave. They knew well that Momma Jane's counterattack was real, it was powerful and it was doing considerable damage to the cause of Christ. The Christians, day after day, cried out to God for more power.

Was Momma Jane's Sorcery Too Much?

God answered by bringing Thomas Muthee and his congregation to a place of desperation. The power of evil had invaded the church to the point that they could hardly pray. One day it got so bad that they started a worship song and were never able to finish it! Something was going on! They went outside and found the remains of fresh places of sacrifices and rituals left behind by Momma Jane.

After that, Thomas Muthee went before the Lord, crying in agony. Was this work going to fail? Was Kiambu truly a graveyard of pastors? Would his spiritual tombstone be added to the others? By this time, Muthee was thoroughly convinced that the demonic powers entrusted to Momma Jane had been the very forces that had driven pastor after pastor out of Kiambu. "God," he prayed, "Do not let me be the next to go—show me the way forward!"

God answered this prayer in a still, small voice by simply suggesting: "My son, I want you to get intercessors on the job."

Fortunately, Thomas understood what God meant. He realized that although he had a congregation of many, many prayers, he had not recognized, designated, empowered and released intercessors. Just as all Christians are expected to be witnesses for

Christ and of them only a few are chosen by God to be evangelists, so all Christians are expected to be pray-ers, but only a few
of them are chosen to be intercessors. This is another one of
those important components of a full-orbed prayer ministry I
have included later on in a whole chapter (chapter 7).

Not wanting to make a mistake or stretch the time line,
Thomas came right to the point and said, "Lord, I am ready to
do it. Who are the intercessors You have chosen?" Remarkably,
God immediately answered and told him five intercessors had
been selected at the present time. He also gave Thomas their
names!

One approach might have been to bring the five together to
fast and pray once a week. A much more radical strategy
seemed to be called for, though. Muthee assigned each intercessor to fast and pray for a whole day, then another for the
next day and so on. That way, one of the intercessors was
always fasting and praying.

Intercessors Need Armor Bearers

The initial results seemed to be positive, but the intercessors
began suffering serious attacks. On their designated fasting
days, sickness and other things debilitated them and prevented
their prayers from being as powerful as they should be. Pastor
Thomas asked the Lord to reveal what should be done, and
God took him to the biblical story of Jonathan, who, unlike
King Saul, went to war having an armor bearer at his side.
Through this seemingly trivial detail, God showed Thomas that
each intercessor needed armor bearers on the specific day designated for fasting and praying.

Thomas called together his intercessors, who by then had
grown to a team of nine, and told them that each person who
was designated to fast on a particular day would be covered by
two armor bearers. One would be the person who had fasted
and prayed the day before, and the other would be the one who

was scheduled to fast and pray the following day. These two would form a protective hedge of prayer around the one on duty.

They did it, and it worked! The spiritual harassment suddenly stopped. The armor-bearer plan has been in place ever since, and at this writing the intercession team has grown to 400 highly committed individuals. Instead of only 1 intercessor fasting and praying each day, they are now divided into blocks of 15 or 20, which means that every single day either 15 or 20 are praying and have a prayer shield spread over each one by two other intercessors.

In Thomas Muthee's opinion, adding the serious intercessors to the prayer ministry of The Prayer Cave was the decisive turning point in the spiritual battle for Kiambu. An increasing number of Momma Jane's clients were becoming Christians and publicly burning the charms and fetishes she had sold them. The way was now open for Muthee to issue a public ultimatum: *"Momma Jane either gets saved and serves the Lord or she leaves town! There is no longer room in Kiambu for both of us!"* In plain terms, Thomas Muthee had challenged Momma Jane to a power encounter, much as Elijah had challenged the priests of Baal.

The Power Encounter

By now the word was spreading around to the city officials that Momma Jane did not seem to have the power she used to have. Her clients were embarrassing her by openly burning fetishes and renouncing curses. Some began pointing out that it could be no coincidence that her Emmanuel Clinic was right next to the area where the serious accidents were occurring. The whole process was brought to a climax when three young children were killed in one of the mysterious accidents. The people of the city were furious. They suspected that it was Momma Jane's black magic that was causing the accidents. They wanted to stone her!

The police were called in and they entered Momma Jane's house to investigate. In one room of the house they were startled to find one of the largest pythons they had ever seen. They immediately shot the snake and killed it. That natural act caused the spiritual battle to end. Momma Jane was taken by the police for questioning and was later released. She quickly and wisely opted to leave town for good. Instead of a preacher's graveyard, Kiambu had miraculously been transformed to a witch's graveyard!

Let's not lose the significance of the snake. That was the event in the *visible* world that reflected what had been happening in the *invisible* world. Before he had arrived in Kiambu, Thomas Muthee had been informed by God that Witchcraft was the principality ruling the city, supported by any number of lesser spirits. Witchcraft's human vehicle was the witch, Momma Jane, who had blasphemed God by calling her den of iniquity "Emmanuel Clinic." She had also become the most powerful woman in Kiambu.

When the apostle Paul arrived in Philippi, he encountered a similar situation. The most spiritually powerful woman in Philippi was a slave girl "possessed with a spirit of divination [or witchcraft]" (Acts 16:16). The details were different, but after a time, Paul also provoked a power encounter and said to the spirit, "I command you in the name of Jesus Christ to come out of her" (v. 18). The slave girl immediately lost her magical powers, many miracles took place and a strong church was planted in Philippi.

What about the snake? Most of our translations use the phrase "spirit of divination" or "spirit of clairvoyance," which is the *functional* name of the territorial spirit over Philippi. Biblical scholars, however, tell us that a more literal rendering of the Greek would give the spirit a *proper* name. For example, Simon Kistemaker points out that the best way to translate the Greek is "a spirit, namely a Python."[1] Here is one indication of the relationship of the snake in the visible world to spirits of witchcraft in the invisible world. It is common that in art designed to glorify the demonic, snakes are frequently used to represent witchcraft.

It comes as no surprise, then, to those familiar with spiritual warfare and spiritual mapping that a huge python was found in Momma Jane's house, and that killing the snake was the final blow to her evil power in Kiambu.

Powerful Prayer Can Change a City!

The point I am trying to make in this chapter is that powerful prayer works. Our case study of The Prayer Cave is a convincing example. The spiritual defeat of Momma Jane is convincing enough, but that is not all. What effect has the prayer ministry of The Prayer Cave had on the city of Kiambu as a whole?

When Momma Jane left the city, things began to change quickly and dramatically. The unbelievers in the city also recognize the cause-and-effect relationship between the power encounter and the subsequent changes in the community.

Economically, the city is now prosperous. Government officials, instead of allegedly paying bribes so as not to be assigned to Kiambu, now are said to pay bribes to get the assignment.

The crime and violence associated with the city in the national media is now virtually gone. The chief of police has recently visited Pastor Muthee and told him that because of what he has done to Kiambu, he has been granted permission to preach anywhere at any time, he can use any volume on the loudspeakers and does not need a permit. Some of the most notorious criminals of the city are now saved and are members of The Prayer Cave. One of the worst drug dealers has renounced such behavior and is enrolled in the church Bible school; he plays bass guitar in the worship team, and he uses his spare time to evangelize patients in the hospitals.

Alcoholism is notably diminished in Kiambu. The intercessors went on prayerwalks around the barrooms, and the loud music is a thing of the past. One of the most prominent high-volume discos is now a church! A small valley near the city had been notorious as a den of bootleggers, producing and selling native beer on the black market. The intercessors targeted it for prayerwalking. The still is now closed, and The Prayer Cave has purchased the land to build its new church facility!

What about the mysterious automobile accidents? As you

Do not forget the central cause of the awesome changes in the city of Kiambu, Kenya: powerful prayer.

---

might have guessed, no such accidents have occurred since the day on which the symbolic python was destroyed and Witchcraft was defeated!

Finally the kingdom of God is coming to Kiambu. No more hostility is present among Christian pastors. Repentance and reconciliation is the order of the day. Churches of all denominations across the city are now growing rapidly, the same as they have in other parts of Kenya. Pastors regularly eat together and pray together. At this writing, they are making plans for the first joint evangelistic citywide crusade that Kiambu has ever known.

Do not forget the central cause of these awesome changes in the city of Kiambu, Kenya: *powerful prayer.*

PRAYER POWER IN ARGENTINA

Momma Jane got off easy, compared to two cases of powerful prayer in Argentina. My wife, Doris, and I have been working with Ed Silvoso, author of *That None Should Perish* (Regal Books), in Argentina for many years. The first season of ministry was in the city of Resistencia in northern Argentina. One of the territorial spirits that had Resistencia under its control was San La Muerte, the spirit of death. Multitudes worshiped this spirit because it promised them "a good death."

Think of the desperation and hopelessness that must have been present in the hearts of those people to grasp hold of such a promise! Death was worshiped in 13 shrines around the city. Many people would take one of its images, carved from human bone, and have it surgically implanted under their skin so that no matter where they went they would be assured of a good death!

A great deal of fervent prayer began to be offered in Resistencia after seminars about intercession were taught by Doris, Cindy Jacobs, Argentine Pastor Eduardo Lorenzo and others. When the time came for the climactic evangelistic event, Doris and Cindy flew to Resistencia and were met with a startling piece of news. The week before they arrived, the high priestess of the cult of San La Muerte had been smoking in bed. She fell asleep, her bed caught on fire, and only three things were consumed by the flames: her mattress, herself and her statue of San La Muerte, which was in another room! Nothing else in the house was touched. The one who had promised others a good death, herself died a horrible death!

Needless to say, the harvest was great in Resistencia. In a short time, the number of believers there had increased by 102 percent! The spirit of death was defeated by powerful prayer, and the kingdom of God poured through Resistencia.

CONFRONTING WITCHCRAFT IN MAR DEL PLATA

The other incident in Argentina took place in the resort city of Mar del Plata. After careful planning and painstaking spiritual mapping, Doris, Cindy, Eduardo Lorenzo and others felt led to take a team of local pastors and intercessors to pray in the central plaza of the city after conducting a prayer and spiritual warfare seminar. They prayed for a couple of hours, asking God to break the spiritual strongholds there. As they were praying out loud, specifically against the spirit of witchcraft, which they had discerned was the major principality over the city, several noticed that the bells in the cathedral rang for a considerable period of time at exactly 4:00 P.M.

The news did not reach them until the next day, when they heard from one of the pastors who had attended the seminar but felt led to pray at home rather than go to the plaza. This pastor's home happened to be right across the street from the home of a Macumba witch of Mar del Plata, the one who had boasted of joining other witches in launching spiritual attacks against the Christian pastors of the city. Shortly after 4:00 P.M., the pastor saw an ambulance pull up to the witch's house and carry her away, dead. She had been in fine health, but witnesses said that she suddenly dropped dead at 4:00 P.M. for no apparent cause!

Cindy Jacobs comments about the incident: "We were stunned when we heard this report. While we were not happy that the woman had died, we were acutely aware that God was sending a clear message of judgment against witchcraft."[2]

WHY DOES PRAYER MAKE A DIFFERENCE?

In the case in Mar del Plata, the *attitude* of God against witchcraft had not been changed by the prayer action in the plaza. Had it not been for the prayer, however, witchcraft in Mar del Plata would have been business as usual, at least according to my best understanding of the theology of prayer. The prayer in the plaza was targeted, it was aggressive, it was empowered by the Holy Spirit and it was intentional. It was an

Elijah kind of prayer. Exactly the same thing could be said about the prayer in Resistencia and in Kiambu, Kenya. In each case, prayer moved the hand of God to show His power in the visible world. Although prayer did not change God's *attitude,* it did influence His *actions.*

How does the prayer action of human beings relate to the sovereignty of God? This is a key issue in understanding the difference between prayer in general and *effective, fervent* prayer.

When I was first moving deeply into my study and understanding of prayer some years ago, one of the statements that helped me most was a chapter title in Jack Hayford's book *Prayer Is Invading the Impossible:* "If We Don't, He Won't." Jack Hayford did not say, "If we don't, He *can't.*" That would have been terrible theology. God is sovereign and He can do anything He wants to do. The sovereign God, however, apparently has chosen to order His creation in such a way that many of His actions are contingent on the prayers of His people. It is as if God has a Plan A He will implement if believers pray. If they do not, He has a Plan B. Plan A is obviously better for all concerned than Plan B. The choice, according to God's design, is ours. If we choose to pray and if we pray powerfully, more blessing will come and God's kingdom will be manifested here on earth in a more glorious way than if we choose not to.

I love the way one of the great scholars of prayer of our generation, Richard Foster, puts it: "We are working with God to determine the future. Certain things will happen in history if we pray rightly."[3]

Any who might doubt this need only ask Thomas Muthee or Cindy Jacobs or, for that matter Momma Jane—to dispel doubts and to build faith that powerful prayer can, indeed, determine the history of our cities and nations.

■ REFLECTION QUESTIONS ■

1. Talk about the suggestion that some prayer is powerful while other prayer may not be. Why don't we hear very many sermons about this?
2. See if you can name two or three tangible answers to your prayer or the prayer of someone you know. Could you prove a scientific cause-and-effect relationship between the prayer and the supposed answer?
3. Thomas Muthee discovered that the territorial spirit over his city was named "Witchcraft." Can you tell of another such case in which the name of a spirit over an area became known?
4. Some people might not believe that the spirits where Momma Jane served would have enough power to cause mysterious accidents in a certain place. What do you think?

Notes

1. Simon J. Kistemaker, *Exposition of the Acts of the Apostles* (Grand Rapids: Baker Book House, 1990), p. 594.
2. Cindy Jacobs, *Possessing the Gates of the Enemy* (Grand Rapids: Baker Book House, 1991; revised edition, 1994), p. 103.
3. Richard Foster, *Celebration of Discipline* (San Francisco: HarperSanFrancisco, 1988), p. 35.

FURTHER RESOURCES

- *And God Changed His Mind* by Brother Andrew and Susan DeVore Williams (Grand Rapids: Chosen Books, 1991). This is one of my favorite books about prayer. Do not miss the chapter titled "When It's Satan's Will, Not God's."
- *Prayer Is Invading the Impossible* by Jack Hayford (New York: Ballantine Books, 1994). A no-nonsense

straightforward look at prayer as a weapon of spiritual warfare.

- *Warfare Prayer* by C. Peter Wagner (Ventura, Calif.: Regal Books, 1992). This first book in *The Prayer Warrior Series* provides more details about the experiment on spiritual warfare in Argentina.
- *Why Pray?* by B. J. Willhite (Altamonte Springs, Fla.: Creation House, 1988). This book contains excellent lessons about why some prayer is more powerful than other prayer.

Two-Way Prayer: Hearing God

CORRIE TEN BOOM'S NAME HAS BECOME A HOUSEHOLD word among many Christians because of her exemplary life of faith while in a Nazi prison camp in Holland. She tells a story that is simple, but at the same time a profound illustration of what I like to call "two-way prayer."

When she was incarcerated in the prison camp, one day she caught a severe cold and was distraught because she had no handkerchief. She told her sister, Betsie, who was a prisoner with her, that she desperately needed a handkerchief, and said, "What can I do?"

Betsie said, "You can pray!" When she saw that Corrie's only response was a patronizing smile, Betsie took matters into her own hands and prayed, "Father, Corrie has a cold and has no handkerchief. Will you please give her one? In Jesus' name. Amen."

Soon after this, Corrie heard her name called. At the

window was a friend who worked in the prison hospital. She handed Corrie a little package, which Corrie opened and was astounded to find a handkerchief! "Why did you bring this?" Corrie asked her friend. "How did you know I had a cold?"

"I had no idea," her friend said. "But while I was folding handkerchiefs in the hospital, a voice in my heart said, 'Take one to Corrie ten Boom.'"

Corrie ten Boom's comment was: "What a miracle! Can you understand what that handkerchief told me at that moment? It told me that in heaven there is a loving Father who hears when one of his children on this very small planet asks for an impossible little thing—a handkerchief. And that heavenly Father tells one of his other children to take a handkerchief to Corrie ten Boom."[1]

Think back for a moment to Thomas Muthee at his lowest point in Kiambu, Kenya, when God told him that the only way forward was to build a team of intercessors. Muthee, like Corrie ten Boom's sister, Betsie, prayed a simple prayer: "Lord, I am ready to do it. Who are the intercessors you have chosen?" As an answer, God gave Thomas *the names* of the five intercessors He had chosen for the pastor.

CAN WE HEAR THE VOICE OF GOD?

The preceding stories are two vivid examples of individuals hearing the voice of God as part of their prayer lives. I chose these two stories because they are uncomplicated. The prayers were direct and unemotional. One was prayed by a pastor and the other by a layperson; one by a black man and the other by a white woman. They experienced no flashing lights or feelings of ecstasy or angelic appearances or sounds of a rushing mighty wind. In both cases, a loving Father spoke to His children in a small, quiet voice. In one case, He spoke back to the person who prayed and in the other He spoke to a third party.

Those to whom He spoke had spiritual ears to hear, combined with the will to obey what they heard. The result? Great blessing!

Furthermore, the voice of God in both of these incidents was so clear and so specific that there could be no question about its source. Granted, sometimes the voice of God is a bit vague; sometimes He speaks in parables that may need interpretation; sometimes He gives us a partial response and expects us to be patient before receiving the rest of it. In the case of the handkerchief, though, for example, God gave a specific command to be implemented immediately in a specific way. No room is found for error here!

This is the way prayer should be. As I have mentioned previously, the essence of prayer is a personal relationship between two persons, or intimacy with the Father. Our relationship with God is not just a close friendship; it is family. I love my pastor, Ted Haggard, for example, and he loves me. He sometimes refers to the 6,000 members of New Life Church, which he pastors, as a "family." This, however, is a metaphor, not to be taken literally. Ted Haggard has a literal family and their primary meeting place is not the church, but his home. Because I have never been in that home, nor do I know where it is, I obviously do not belong to his family. I have never seen Pastor Ted in his pajamas!

MEETING GOD IN THE LIVING ROOM

God, however, tells us that He is our Father. When we talk to Him, we talk to Him as if we both were in the living room of our own house. I had a wonderful relationship with my own father, who is now with the Lord. During the last 15 years of his life, he lived in Massachusetts and I lived in California. I made a habit of calling him on the telephone every Sunday. When I called him, I did not expect to talk and talk and talk and then hang up. I expected to talk a bit and then listen to what my father had to say and then go on from there. This is the most natural thing for a father and his son.

Why would we expect differently from our heavenly Father? Too often our prayer lives are conducted as if heaven were a big telephone bank we call and leave voice mail for God. That is not what God wants. He wants us listening and able to hear when He says something such as, "Give Corrie ten Boom a handkerchief."

I like the way Pastor Bill Hybels of Willow Creek Community Church in South Barrington, Illinois, puts it: "You can't build a relationship on one-way speeches. You need frequent, sustained, intimate contact between two persons, both of whom speak and both of whom listen....Listening to God speak through His Holy Spirit is not only normal; it is essential."[2]

I must admit that I did not always know this. The Christian circles in which I moved did not stress two-way prayer. For years, I was not at a place where I could have heard the voice of God as did Thomas Muthee or Corrie's friend. It did not matter that I was an ordained minister and a seminary professor and an author of several Christian books. No one had taught me in seminary what I am teaching in this chapter.

Learning to hear the voice of God was a long process for me because it was such a radical departure from my past. Among my circle of close friends and trusted colleagues, the one who first began to hear God's voice clearly, as I recall, was John Wimber. He encouraged me to begin experimenting a bit in distinguishing between my own thoughts and what the Father was attempting to speak into me. As I was working my way through this concept, I will never forget the effect of a statement made by Pastor Jack Hayford as I was reading *Glory on Your House*, the book he wrote about his church, The Church On The Way, in Van Nuys, California.

"AND I QUOTE"

Hayford writes, "And yet when I say that the Lord has spoken to me, I mean something even more specific than general revelation or private inner impressions. I reserve these words intentionally for the rare, special occasions when, in my spirit, I have had the Lord speak directly to me. I do not mean, 'I felt impressed,' or 'I sensed somehow.' Instead, I mean that at a given moment, almost always when I have least expected it, the Lord spoke *words* to me. Those words have been so distinct that I feel virtually able to say, 'And I quote.'"[3]

It is safe to say that the majority of those reading this chapter will, at this point, agree that we can and should practice two-way prayer and listen to the voice of God. Not all, however, will agree. Jack Hayford may have convinced me, but he has not convinced everyone else that we can indeed hear the very words of God.

As a matter of fact, growing evidence reveals that this issue may be one of the last remaining major barriers between charismatics and traditional evangelicals. After we agree on levels of tolerance relating to such things as praying for the sick, casting out demons, speaking in tongues, raising hands in church and falling down under the power of the Spirit, hearing the direct voice of God is still a nonnegotiable issue for some.

A MAJOR BARRIER?

Speaking of Jack Hayford, he recently took a giant step in helping to remove barriers between charismatics and traditional evangelicals when he wrote *The Beauty of Spiritual Language;* the whole book focuses on speaking in tongues. In it, he naturally raises the issue, dear to the hearts of classical Pentecostals and others, of whether speaking in tongues is to be regarded as the initial physical evidence of receiving the bap-

tism in the Holy Spirit. His conclusion, based on his understanding of the Bible, is that those who have suggested that
speaking in tongues is the initial physical evidence have built
"an unintended but nonetheless restrictive barrier."[4] Hayford
believes, as noncharismatic evangelicals have long contended,
that evidences other than speaking in tongues may verify a
believer is filled with the Holy Spirit.

Soon after Hayford published his book, Pastor Chuck Swindoll was invited to become the president of Dallas Theological
Seminary, an institution widely known for its serious concerns
about Pentecostal/charismatic theology and practice. *Christianity Today* magazine conducted a substantial interview with
Chuck Swindoll and the interviewer kept probing areas that
might uncover possible changes Swindoll would implement
once he became president. Swindoll was diplomatically non-
committal in his responses until the interviewer posed the following question:

"In *The Beauty of Spiritual Language* Jack Hayford says that
speaking in tongues is not necessarily a precondition for fullness in the Spirit. If that's the case, what are the barriers
between evangelicals and charismatics?"

Swindoll's response, coming from such a highly respected
evangelical leader, will leave no doubt that hearing from God
remains a central issue to many: "The *primary* barrier would be
extrabiblical revelation. Now, Jack's a good friend, and I love
him dearly. He's taught me as much about worship as anyone
else. But I think he would have room in his theology for extrabiblical revelation, *of God speaking outside the Scriptures and
beyond the Scriptures.* I have trouble with that" (italics mine).[5]

JACK DEERE'S PARADIGM SHIFT

The best response to this key question about whether we can
receive valid information from God outside the Scriptures, in

my opinion, comes from Jack Deere, who for many years served a distinguished career as an Old Testament professor at Dallas Theological Seminary.

During Deere's time at the Seminary, he taught his students that God did not engage in present-day revelatory activities. God's revelation was contained in the 66 books of the Bible, and hearing God's voice today means correctly exegeting the Scriptures. A tacit understanding existed among him and several of his colleagues that regarded it as disreputable behavior to attribute the reason they had decided to do or say a certain thing as "God told me to." Those who wished to be more technical labeled such a statement as "dangerous epistemology."

Five years before Chuck Swindoll became president of Dallas Seminary, Jack Deere was forced to leave the faculty because he had undergone a paradigm shift and broke seminary taboos by attending a Vineyard Christian Fellowship church. No longer a cessationist (believing that the miraculous gifts of the Spirit ceased with the Apostolic Age), he was regarded as incompatible with one of the seminary's major tenets of faith. Deere subsequently wrote a masterful book, *Surprised by the Power of the Spirit*, in which he defends contemporary ministries of healing, deliverance and miracles. When he originally outlined the book, he had planned on including a section about hearing the voice of God. Instead, he mentioned it only in an epilogue.

Why?

As Deere searched the Scriptures, prayed fervently and organized his thoughts about hearing from God, he says, "[One] chapter quickly became two chapters, then three, and then I realized that I had begun another book altogether."[6] As a background to this, he reveals to his readers, "The most difficult transition for me in my pilgrimage was not in accepting that Scripture teaches that God heals and does miracles today through gifted believers. The thing I resisted the most, was most afraid of, and which took the most convincing was accepting that God still *speaks* today" (italics his).[7]

The result of this process was the publication of a second book, 80 pages longer than the first one, which, at least in my opinion, should put to rest all biblical, theological, historical and epistemological arguments against the possibility of God's speaking and our hearing His voice today: *Surprised by the Voice of God.*

No reputable Christian leaders we know who believe that God speaks today would ever equate anything they hear or that others hear with Scripture.

Jack Deere and I both agree that the *motivation* in the hearts of those who do not believe in present-day divine revelation is a commendable motivation. We join them in the heartfelt desire to affirm the unique authority of the written Word of God in the Bible. Thinking back, Deere says the thing that frightened him the most was this: "If I admitted that God was still speaking apart from the Bible, wouldn't I be opening the canon of Scripture again?"[8]

Jack now realizes that his was an unfounded fear because no reputable Christian leaders we know who believe that God speaks today would ever equate anything they hear or that others hear with Scripture. He sums it up by saying, "Today, after years of practical experience and intense study on the subject of God's speaking, I am convinced that God does indeed speak apart from the Bible, *though never in contradiction to it*" (italics mine).[9]

PROPHECIES AND PROPHETS

Up till now, I have not used the term "prophecy," although it is directly related to two-way prayer and hearing the voice of God. If God does not speak today, there are, by definition, no longer any prophets. Prophecy has the distinction of being one of only two spiritual gifts (the other one being teaching) that are mentioned in all three primary lists of gifts: 1 Corinthians 12, Romans 12 and Ephesians 4. I define prophecy as follows: "The gift of prophecy is the special ability that God gives to certain members of the Body of Christ to receive and communicate an immediate message of God to His people through a divinely anointed utterance."[10]

We live in a time when prophecy is becoming more and more recognized throughout the Body of Christ. The argument that God does not speak outside of the Bible may well belong on some "endangered doctrine" list. The best I can calculate, the resurgence of biblical prophecy and the prophetic movement began around 1980 and has been picking up speed ever since.

Jack Deere's is not the only book helping spur this movement along. Professor Wayne Grudem of Trinity Evangelical Divinity School in Deerfield, Illinois, has provided solid biblical foundations in *The Gift of Prophecy in the New Testament and Today* (Crossway Books). One of the most helpful books to me during my paradigm shift in the 1980s was *Prophets and Personal Prophecy* (Destiny Image Publishers) by Bill Hamon, president of the Christian International Network.

Mike Bickle, pastor of the Kansas City Metro Christian Fellowship, is regarded by many as the nation's foremost pastor to prophets. He shares his wisdom, refined through many years, in *Growing in the Prophetic*. One of the most highly recommended books by practitioners active in prophetic ministries is *The Voice of God* by Cindy Jacobs.

The combination of scholar, theologian and theoretician, Jack

Deere, along with intercessor and practitioner, Cindy Jacobs, is notable. The two together, both good friends of mine, provide a dependable compass point for those who desire to explore the path of contemporary prophecy, still a rather unfamiliar journey for many, including me. I love the titles of these two books, which were published within a year of each other. Jack, the former cessationist, is *Surprised by the Voice of God*. Cindy, who has been hearing from God since she was four, was not surprised at all. She calls her book, simply, *The Voice of God*.

THE NEW APOSTOLIC REFORMATION

I am giving considerable emphasis to prophecy on these pages because I sense we are living in the midst of an extraordinary move of God. It has recently become evident that the fastest growing segment of Christianity on six continents is a movement I call the New Apostolic Reformation. It includes, among many others, African Independent Churches, Chinese house churches, Latin American grassroots churches, independent charismatics and many local congregations still operating within traditional denominational structures. One of the most innovative characteristics of this movement (although several exceptions might exist) is the reinstatement of the New Testament *offices* of prophet and apostle.

Many of these churches have a strong desire to implement, in a practical way, what many of them call "the fivefold ministry" of Ephesians 4:11: apostles, prophets, evangelists, pastors and teachers. Most churches in general, they point out, have functioned for years by using evangelists, pastors and teachers, but for reasons now considered inadequate by the leaders of the New Apostolic Reformation, have decided not to recognize apostles and prophets.

I have mentioned that I believe acceptance of the office of prophet began diffusing rapidly throughout the Body of Christ around 1980. Likewise, I believe reinstatement of the office of apostle began a similar process around 1990. Pastor David Cannistraci of Evangel Christian Fellowship in San Jose, California, has published an excellent textbook, which I use in my classes, *The Gift of Apostle* (Regal Books). Bill Hamon, whom I mentioned earlier, has now written a new book titled *Apostles & Prophets and Coming Moves of God* (Destiny Image Publishers).

RECOGNIZING THE *OFFICE* OF PROPHET

My purpose here, in a chapter called "Two-Way Prayer: Hearing God," is to explain the office of prophet. Because this is new to much of the contemporary Church, it is expected that for some time certain issues will be discussed and debated and various leaders will come to various conclusions. One of these issues is whether titles such as Apostle So-and-So or Prophet So-and-So should be used.

The discussion is not so much whether the functions or ministries of apostles and prophets should be recognized, but whether individuals should formally be set into the offices and use titles as we do for the other Ephesians 4:11 offices, such as Evangelist Billy Graham or Pastor Robert Schuller or Professor/Doctor Peter Wagner.

Mike Bickle is among the more cautious. His church, the spiritual home of what some have called the "Kansas City Prophets," was strongly criticized in the media awhile ago by some who had not yet come to terms with high-visibility prophetic ministry. Bickle has therefore tried to develop a way of communicating in the least offensive way possible, and so he says, "I'm not at all comfortable with labeling most people who prophesy as 'prophets.'"[11]

Instead, Bickle classifies "prophetically gifted people" in his church on four levels: Level One: "Simple Prophetic"; Level Two: "Prophetic Gifting"; Level Three: "Prophetic Ministry"; and

Level Four: "Prophetic Office."[12] He clearly does not deny the existence of the prophetic office, but he says few people he knows personally (and he knows more potential "prophets" than most) qualify for such a designation.

As a matter of fact, Mike Bickle says, "I think the church does itself harm when it allows people to quickly identify themselves as 'apostle' or 'prophet' simply because they consider themselves to be so."[13]

Cindy Jacobs agrees. She says, "Years before I was actually set into the office of the prophet, people would often ask me, 'Are you a prophetess?' Each time they would ask, I would reply in return, 'No I'm not a prophetess. I'll know when He sets me into the office.'"[14] It is one thing for individuals to recognize the fact that they hear from God more frequently and more accurately than most. It is quite another, however, to add to that the godly character and matured wisdom, as Mike Bickle says, that causes peers to agree that the person merits the designation of "prophet."

This eventually happened to Cindy Jacobs in a time of powerful corporate intercession when she heard the voice of God say to her heart: "Cindy, this night I set you in as a prophetess to the nations." She herself might not have announced this to others except that the leader of the meeting later began to pray specifically for Cindy and, among other things, prophesied personally to her: "And the Lord says, 'This night I stand you up as a prophetess to the nations.'"

Jacobs says, "In ways that are hard to describe, I was different from that night forward."[15] Even so, she prefers not to use the title "Prophet" or "Prophetess"; mainly to avoid misunderstandings on the part of believers who are not yet sure the New Testament office of prophet is valid today. I think that in a relatively short period of time this inhibition will largely evaporate.

GOD COMMUNICATES IN VARIOUS WAYS

When we practice two-way prayer, expecting to hear God, we must be prepared to "hear" Him in various ways. God has not chosen to limit Himself to verbal communication. Jack Deere clarifies this as thoroughly as anyone I know. He explains that God at times uses supernatural means to speak to us, such as what Deere calls the audible voice: the voice audible to you alone, the internal audible voice and the voice of angels. God also uses natural means such as dreams, visions, trances, sentence fragments, single words, impressions and human messengers.[16]

My own experiences in hearing God are the more sedate kind. I have yet to hear the audible voice of God or to receive divine communication through a dream or a vision. As I pray every morning, for example, I try to pause from time to time to see what God may bring to my mind. More and more I think I am able to know it when it happens. I want to be one of the sheep that knows the Shepherd's voice. On other occasions, rather infrequently I must admit, the power of God seems to come on me in a rather special way, and I am sure that what is coming through my mind is none other than the voice of God.

This happened, for example, when I was preparing to write *Churches That Pray*, the third volume of *The Prayer Warrior Series*. It was such a clear experience that I can still remember where it happened: in a motel room in Portland, Oregon. In that motel room, God spoke to me and told me I was not to write *Churches That Pray* as yet because I was not ready. Instead, I was to add a volume about spiritual mapping as the fourth in what was at first projected to be a three-volume series.

This is admittedly a paraphrase, but here is the way I remember it: God said, "I want you to write a book on spiritual mapping."

I said, "But, God, I don't know enough about spiritual mapping to write a whole book on it."

"I know that," He replied, "but you now know the people who do know enough. You know enough to write one chapter, and the others will write the rest of the book."

As soon as God said this, I knew He was referring to the people with whom I was by then in touch through serving as the coordinator of the International Spiritual Warfare Network. I took out my yellow pad, began to write under a special anointing of the Holy Spirit, and in probably less than a half hour I had written the outline of what resulted in *Breaking Strongholds in Your City*. This is the first time I had ever received the vision and design for a book through directly hearing the voice of God. So far it has been the only time.

This does not mean *Breaking Strongholds in Your City* is a book written under divine inspiration. Once again I say that receiving a word from God must never be confused with Scripture or put on a plane equal to Scripture. To prove it, let me make a confession. I firmly believe I heard the voice of God in the motel room, but I was only 90 percent accurate. In my original outline I had included 10 chapters, but later God showed me, this time through trusted colleagues instead of a direct voice that, although the manuscript had been written, edited and designed, I was to remove one chapter and the end result was to be only nine. Removing it was a painful process I might have avoided had my spiritual ears been more finely tuned at the time.

INDIVIDUAL OR CORPORATE?

Experience has shown that some who are just beginning to realize two-way prayer is a reality and God does, indeed, speak to us today, prefer to limit hearing God in an individual's own situation rather than in a corporate sense. They draw a line when some believe they may be receiving a message from God that applies to another person, to a group, to a ministry, to a church, to a city, to a nation or whatever.

Mike Bickle describes this well. He says, "Usually people have no problem with the woman in the prayer group who feels a burden to pray for someone, who senses the Holy Spirit leading her prayer, and who states that God is 'impressing' something on her heart....But if she speaks up during the Sunday morning service...and loudly proclaims her revelation interspersed with 'Thus saith the Lord,' she could get a significantly

---

It is important to recognize that God's response to two-way prayer can be corporate as well as individual.

---

different response." That is putting it mildly. Some churches I know would give her the legendary right foot of fellowship if she did it too often. Although, as Bickle says, "Here are the same words and the same message, but delivered in a very different package."[17]

It is important to recognize that God's response to two-way prayer can be corporate as well as individual. I like the subtitle of Cindy Jacobs's book *The Voice of God.* It says: *How God Speaks* Personally *and* Corporately *to His Children Today.* If personally, it can be for a general direction or for a specific situation. Believers seem to have less problem for the general direction kind of word than for the specific situation kind of word.

A biblical example for a general direction would be the well-known "Macedonian Call." This time God used a vision to communicate with Paul. A man from Macedonia appeared and said, simply, "Come over to Macedonia and help us" (Acts 16:9). This was all Paul needed to take his church-planting team to Macedonia. He was particularly ready for such a clear word because just before this he thought the Lord was calling him to Asia and he was wrong. Then he thought the Lord was calling him to Bithynia and he was wrong again. I must say it is comforting to know that even the famous apostle Paul did not hear the Lord correctly every time.

A more specific individual word came through an angel to Philip when he was in the midst of a revival in Samaria: "Arise and go toward the south along the road which goes down from Jerusalem to Gaza" (Acts 8:26). Philip obeyed, he saw a chariot, and this time the Holy Spirit, not an angel, said, "Go near and overtake this chariot" (v. 29). Such "quote-unquote" words appear enough in the Bible to lead many of us to believe that God might do that very thing today. Let me give you a fascinating example.

DEATH TO MORRIS CERULLO

My friend Morris Cerullo tells of an incident in Haiti some years ago when hearing the voice of God may well have saved his life. He had been invited to conduct an evangelistic campaign there by none other than François "Papa Doc" Duvalier, the dictator at the time. When he arrived, he found that all the posters advertising the crusade had been torn down by the voodoo witch doctors, taken to their homes and stuck with pins to seal the voodoo curses against him. He was met at the airport by a large group of senators, businesspeople and other dignitaries. The government had provided a full motorcade to take him past the presidential palace and then to his hotel.

The moment he settled into the backseat of the lead limousine, Morris Cerullo developed a horrible pain in the pit of his stomach. It got worse and worse until it became totally unbearable. He said to his song leader next to him, "Tell the driver to get out of this motorcade and take me to the hotel."

"He can't do it," was the reply. "The president has ordered us to pass by his palace."

Cerullo raised his voice enough to startle a senator who was sitting in the front seat: "Get me out of here! Don't ask any questions!" The automobile turned off on the next street and sped to the hotel.

Once in his room, Cerullo fell prostrate on the floor in a soaking sweat. His prayer was a very simple one: "God, what is going on?"

He then heard the voice of God, who said, "Son, I have allowed this to happen for a reason. I wanted to get you out of the motorcade and have your full attention so that I could talk to you." At that point the pain suddenly and totally left Morris's body!

Still stretched out on the floor, Cerullo said, "What is it you want to tell me, God?"

"I wanted to tell you that tonight 300 witch doctors are coming to your meeting to kill you!"

Morris replied, "That's fine. I am consecrated to death. Now what am I supposed to do? Do you want me to die as a martyr?"

God said, "No. Instead, I am going to tell you how to identify them," at which point God proceeded to show him the color of their clothing and exactly how to pick the individual voodoo witch doctors out of the crowd. Then God said, "Son, tonight the words that you speak will be as if I have spoken them. I will bring to pass what you speak." This is as clear a directive word from God for a specific situation that I could imagine. What happened?

The Challenge of a Power Encounter

When Morris Cerullo stood up to speak in front of the 15,000 people in the stadium, he soon noticed that here and there all over the audience certain individuals were beginning to sing chants in a soft voice. Cerullo called for order and they stopped. Soon they started again, and this scenario repeated itself several times. The pitch of the battle in the invisible world was increasing rapidly. The Creole interpreter, a Bible school student, was so terrified that he wet his pants! At the highest point of tension, Cerullo was ready for the power encounter, much as Elijah had been on Mount Carmel.

"People of Haiti," he announced, "There are hundreds of witch doctors here tonight. They have come to kill me. You say, 'How do you know?' I know because the living God has told me. Now you witch doctors, listen to me. I know exactly who you are and where you are sitting! The living God has showed you to me!"

Cerullo then started pointing to them one by one, and said, "Tonight we're going to find out whether the devil that you serve or the God whom I serve has more power!" He turned to all the dignitaries and their wives seated on the platform and said, "I will not be responsible for what is going to happen now."

Facing the witch doctors, Cerullo said, "If you open your mouths one more time, I will not be responsible when they carry you out of this meeting dead!" From that moment on not one person chanted, spoke or moved at all.

"My God! That's My Neighbor!"
After Cerullo had preached for 20 minutes, a scream was heard in the back of the stadium. A commotion started, and the crowd passed a little child four or five years old over their heads toward the platform. The interpreter said, "They are shouting that this baby was born blind and now he can see! They sent him up here because they didn't know what else to do."

Soon the mother and father pushed through the crowd and arrived at the platform. Their child had been totally healed! Right then an army general in full regalia who was on the platform literally jumped out of his seat, put his hands on his head, and screamed, "My God! That's my neighbor!"

The crusade stretched out morning, afternoon and evening for three weeks as multitudes came forward to be saved and healed. It was clear to all concerned that the living God whom

Morris Cerullo had come to preach was supremely powerful.[18]

Question: What might have happened if Morris Cerullo had not been prepared, before he went to Haiti, to practice two-way prayer? The magnitude of the potential disaster stretches our imaginations.

CORPORATE WORDS FROM GOD

First Corinthians 14 focuses not on personal prophecy, but on prophetic words given to the whole congregation. Because of the public nature of this kind of ministry, many local churches that encourage the gift of prophecy establish guidelines to maintain order and credibility. Frequently these prophecies are devotional and inspirational. At other times they are directional.

Needless to say, responsible prophets who receive directional words for a church or another such group always check them with the leadership beforehand. If the leaders do not witness positively to the word, saying it in public is not allowed until agreement is reached. In the local church, prophets willingly and humbly submit to the authority of the pastor.

Although I do not pastor a church, my wife, Doris, and I do lead a ministry: Global Harvest Ministries. We had been living in Pasadena, California, for almost a quarter of a century and were intending to spend the rest of our days there. Two of our team of personal intercessors, however, Cindy Jacobs and Jean Steffenson, had on two separate occasions brought us a word from the Lord that we would soon be moving to Colorado Springs. We honestly thought they had missed it just as Paul missed it when he thought he should go to Bithynia. We should have paid more attention to them. We have now moved Global Harvest Ministries to Colorado Springs where we are participating in founding the new World Prayer Center. As a matter of fact, this is the first book I am writing in our new home in Colorado Springs.

The word from God that Cindy and Jean had was a corporate word, which affected the future of a whole ministry, just as words from others can affect a whole church. They were prudent in the way they gave it and they prayed it into fulfillment in God's own time. My wife and I are grateful that these two intercessors, and many others as well, were experienced in practicing two-way prayer. If this has not yet become a part of your prayer life, I hope it does very soon. It will bless you and those around you.

■ REFLECTION QUESTIONS ■

1. Some say that if we believe we can hear the voice of God directly, we open the door to subjectivism and violate the clear words of what has been written in the Bible. In what ways do you agree, and in what ways do you disagree?
2. Prophetic ministry has become common these days. Do you agree that certain people should be recognized as "prophets"? Why?
3. Sometimes God communicates in an audible voice. Have you ever heard of examples of that today?
4. What do you think of people who have prophetic ministries and, from time to time, stand up in church meetings and proclaim to the congregation, "Thus saith the Lord..."?

Notes
1. The story of Corrie ten Boom is paraphrased from *Miracles Happen When You Pray* by Quin Sherrer (Ann Arbor, Mich.: Servant Books, 1996), pp. 23-24 of Part 1 from the manuscript.
2. Bill Hybels, *Too Busy Not To Pray* (Downers Grove, Ill.: InterVarsity Press, 1988), pp. 109-110.
3. Jack Hayford, *Glory on Your House* (Grand Rapids: Chosen Books, 1982; revised edition, 1991), p. 139.
4. Jack Hayford, *The Beauty of Spiritual Language* (Dallas, Tex.: Word Publishing, 1992), p. 92.

5. "Dallas' New Dispensation," Interview by Michael G. Maudlin, *Christianity Today* (October 25, 1993): 15.
6. Jack Deere, *Surprised by the Power of the Spirit* (Grand Rapids: Zondervan Publishing House, 1993), p. 215.
7. Ibid., p. 212.
8. Ibid., p. 213.
9. Ibid., p. 214.
10. For an explanation of this definition, see my book *Your Spiritual Gifts Can Help Your Church Grow* (Ventura, Calif.: Regal Books, 1979; revised edition, 1994), pp. 200-203.
11. Mike Bickle, *Growing in the Prophetic* (Orlando, Fla.: Creation House, 1996), p. 123.
12. Ibid., p. 120.
13. Ibid., p. 123.
14. Cindy Jacobs, *The Voice of God* (Ventura, Calif.: Regal Books, 1995), p. 180.
15. Ibid.
16. Jack Deere, *Surprised by the Voice of God* (Grand Rapids: Zondervan Publishing House, 1996). These forms of hearing from God are explained in chapters 9 and 10.
17. Bickle, *Growing in the Prophetic*, p. 101.
18. The story of Morris Cerullo in Haiti was paraphrased from a video recording of his message given at his Spiritual Warfare School of Ministry in Chicago, July 4, 1996.

FURTHER RESOURCES

- *The Voice of God* by Cindy Jacobs (Ventura, Calif.: Regal Books, 1995). This book is crammed with practical suggestions about how to get in tune with God's voice and how to minister in prophecy.
- *Surprised by the Power of the Spirit* (1993) and *Surprised by the Voice of God* (1996) by Jack Deere (Grand Rapids: Zondervan Publishing House). These two books are doing more than any others to help those rooted in traditional evangelicalism to begin to understand and move with the flow of the Holy Spirit in our generation.
- *Your Spiritual Gifts Can Help Your Church Grow* by C. Peter Wagner (Ventura, Calif.: Regal Books, 1979; revised edition, 1994). This book, the best-selling of all my books, shows how the gift of prophecy fits in with 26 other spiritual gifts designed for ministry in the Church.
- *The Gift of Prophecy in the New Testament and Today*

by Wayne Grudem (Westchester, Ill.: Crossway Books, 1988). A scholarly defense of the validity of the prophetic gift in the churches today.

- *Prophets and Personal Prophecy* by Bill Hamon (Shippensburg, Pa.: Destiny Image Publishers, 1987). This book was my most helpful orientation to the subject of prophecy, once I became convinced that prophecy was for today.
- *Growing in the Prophetic* by Mike Bickle (Orlando, Fla.: Creation House, 1996). As the personal pastor to a number of high-visibility prophets, Mike Bickle has an unusually deep reservoir of understanding and experience to share.

Strategic-Level Intercession

THREE

L ET'S LOOK AT TWO DRAMATIC INCIDENTS ON OPPOSITE sides of the world.

"I'M THE PRINCE OF PERU"

A young Brazilian man named Jesuel is sent out by his local church as a church-planting missionary to neighboring Peru. Soon after he arrives, he is discussing with some friends the strategy they will use to plant their first church. During this discussion, Jesuel reports, a demon calling himself "Prince of Peru" appears to him. The demon says, "Go back to your own land or you will die in Peru!"

Within a week of this confrontation, Jesuel became critically ill. He sought medical care, but the doctors could give him no hope of recovery. They informed him that, although he was young, he needed to face the fact that he was on his deathbed.

As he fought for his life, a nearby pastor, who believed in two-way prayer, was suddenly impressed by God to go to the hospital and pray for a certain young man who was there. He had never heard of Jesuel, nor did he know why this Brazilian might have come to Peru. He obeyed God, though, prayed for Jesuel, and Jesuel was miraculously healed and released from the hospital.

Jesuel then went to a town in northern Peru where, after four weeks of fruitless evangelistic efforts, he discovered that the Catholic church had not been used for six months. He befriended the church's caretaker and led him to Christ. The two of them decided they would ring the church bells and call the townspeople together for a "mass." When the bell rang, people came to the church from all directions and 100 gave their lives to Christ that day.

Many more were saved and nurtured until nearby Catholic priests heard what was going on and put a stop to it. Jesuel, however, simply moved to another place and planted five more churches in Peru before returning to Brazil to be married.[1]

THE "SPIRITUAL TRIANGLE"

One of my students, who must go unnamed, is the leader of his denomination in a certain restricted country. Citizens of his nation are well aware of the "spiritual triangle" formed by lines drawn on a map from the points determined by the location of three particular cities. The power center of the ancient rulers of the nation was located there. It was the place where the government authorities had formally dedicated their nation to a high-ranking spiritual principality. "It is here," says my student, "that the nation's spiritual fate is still decided today."

The human spiritual ruler of the triangle was the abbot of a popular monastery. He was a powerful occult practitioner and a known murderer. Some referred to him as the "killer abbot."

Through the years, the killer abbot and his predecessors had effectively kept any Christian church from being planted in the spiritual triangle. One exception was a Roman Catholic church, which was subsequently burned down. Recently, however, a group of local Christians had felt led by God to conduct an aggressive, high-intensity prayer initiative in the area.

Soon afterward, a pastor moved in to plant a church where churches had been forbidden. Predictably, the abbot confronted the Christian pastor and informed him in no uncertain terms that if he continued in his plans to invade the spiritual triangle, he would pay for his foolishness with his life within a week. The church planter, his faith having been lifted to a high level through the powerful prayer initiative, accepted the challenge and boldly engaged in the obvious power encounter.

Before the end of the week, a terrorist attack (not unusual for this nation at the time) swept through the area, and the abbot himself was killed! At this writing, two Christian churches are now located in the spiritual triangle and one more is being planned. My friend is so encouraged with his nation's new spiritual atmosphere that he believes the 320 churches of his denomination can multiply to 1,000 during the next four years.

SPIRITUAL POWER ON THE HIGHER LEVELS

Case studies involving confrontations with something like a "Prince of Peru" or killer abbots living in triangular spiritual power points take us to levels of spiritual interaction that many of us, including me, had not been introduced to until fairly recently.

I will not soon forget the National Day of Prayer in Washington, D.C., May 1989, when my wife, Doris, and I first became acquainted with Cindy Jacobs and her husband, Mike. As we were being driven to lunch, I casually asked, "What do you do?"

Cindy responded in a rather matter-of-fact way, "We pray for nations."

"How do you pray for nations?" I said, never having heard of anything like that before.

"Well," she said, "we mostly pray for nations just like other people pray for individuals."

Doris and I, whose lives had been dedicated to reaching the nations of the world for Jesus Christ, were intrigued. We invited the Jacobses to sit with us at lunch, and the conversation became one of those rare occasions in which the direction of a career is molded.

Among other things, Cindy explained that if demonic spirits are preventing an *individual* from being all that God wants the person to be, the best approach is to confront the spirits themselves as well as any strongholds that might be providing them legal right to molest the person. Doris and I already knew that, but Cindy continued. She explained that the same principle applies for *groups of people* in cities or nations. Through prayer, such as that practiced through the Jacobses' ministry, Generals of Intercession, and others, spiritual forces on the higher levels can be confronted and weakened or even defeated.

My mind went to 2 Corinthians 4, where Paul expresses his frustration that not enough lost people are being saved through his ministry. He laments that the gospel seems to be "veiled" from those who are lost. Why? Because the "god of this age" has blinded their minds (see vv. 3,4). I had to admit that, as a professional missiologist, I knew all too little about what devices Satan ordinarily uses to keep masses of human minds blinded to the gospel.

Later that year, at the historic Lausanne II in Manila congress on evangelism, several workshops were conducted by some who believed they were beginning to understand more about what these satanic devices to block world evangelism might be. The name frequently used at that time was "territorial spirits." This was the first time most of us who had been rooted in traditional evangelicalism had begun to think about such things, to say nothing of discussing them openly. By that time, I had been learning a bit about how to hear the voice of God, as I explained in the last chapter, and therefore I was ready when He said to me, "I want you to take international leadership in this area of territorial spirits." It was one of the clearest words I have ever received.

The upshot was organizing the International Spiritual Warfare Network, which for years has served as a forum in which issues related to the higher levels of spiritual confrontation have been discussed. Early on, a consensus developed that there were, indeed, various levels of spiritual warfare. Three distinct levels became highlighted and names were assigned.

The Three Levels of Spiritual Warfare

- *Ground-level spiritual warfare* confronts demonic spirits that molest individuals. This is personal deliverance: casting out demons.
- *Occult-level spiritual warfare* exposes organized forces of darkness such as witchcraft, shamanism, satanism, Freemasonry, Eastern religions, New Age and the like.
- *Strategic-level spiritual warfare* involves wrestling with principalities and powers and rulers of the darkness, as Paul defines in Ephesians 6:12.

Although all levels are interrelated in the invisible world and therefore all are important areas of confrontation with evil, my chief personal interest lies with strategic-level spiritual warfare. This seems to me to be the level that promises the greatest payoff for world evangelization. It also demands the greatest risk, therefore it is not for everyone. Nevertheless, "high risk, high return" applies as well here as it does to the business world, in my opinion.

Let me explain why I have such a personal interest in strategic-level spiritual warfare, because I am occasionally misunderstood. Most, I think, would agree that as individuals serving

---

We are primarily responsible for the particular set of gifts, callings, anointings, talents and life situations God has chosen to give us. That constitutes our spiritual DNA, so to speak.

God, we are primarily responsible for the particular set of gifts, callings, anointings, talents and life situations He has chosen to give us. That constitutes our spiritual DNA, so to speak, and no one else in the Body of Christ may be exactly like us. This is why I do not expect everyone else necessarily to think as I think or act as I act or even agree with my opinions.

VARIOUS KINDS OF PRAYER

Those who have read the five books of *The Prayer Warrior Series*, for example, may have noticed that I am not equally interested in every kind of prayer. For example, I intercede, but I am not an intercessor who prays two or three or more hours a day. I fast, but I am not a 40-day or even a 7-day faster. I worship, but I do not indulge in a steady diet of worship tapes on my car stereo. I study Scripture, but I am not a Bible scholar devoted to exegeting the Greek and the Hebrew. I am concerned for the poor and the oppressed, but I am not a social activist.

Therefore, when I read a book such as Richard Foster's classic, which has the straightforward title *Prayer* (HarperSanFrancisco), I find many parts of it boring. Just glancing down the table of contents of what I call, in my lighter moments, the "Cookbook of Prayer," for example, I find myself skipping over "The Prayer of Examen," "The Prayer of Tears," "Sacramental Prayer," "Meditative Prayer," "The Prayer of Suffering," "Contemplative Prayer" or "The Prayer of Relinquishment," just to name a few. They are excellent forms of prayer and dear to the hearts of many believers, but they do not seem to fit my particular spiritual DNA.

I believe that my spiritual genetic code came through the new birth. When I was 19 years of age, I was saved and I was called to be a missionary on the same day, just as the apostle Paul was (see Acts 26:17). I can never remember a day in my Christian life since then when spreading the gospel around the world was not my highest purpose. Therefore, when I began plunging deeply into the prayer movement in the late 1980s, the kinds of prayer that attracted me the most for personal research, writing and teaching were the kinds of prayer that showed the most cause-and-effect promise for evangelization. I found myself working mostly with prayer that could be regarded as a *means to the end* of evangelization, not with many other kinds of prayer, good as they may be, that tend to be considered as *ends in themselves.*

No two people have gained higher respect in the prayer movement of our nation than my friends Evelyn Christenson and David Bryant. Evelyn says, "We must be very careful not to substitute the means for the end. Our means—our ministry—should become the stepping stones, the open doors, for actual evangelizing....*Prayer* is a very important *means* in the salvation process" (italics hers).[2]

David Bryant argues that united prayer efforts such as Concerts of Prayer can be powerful occasions for spiritual warfare, but, he says, "Revival praying, biblically understood, is the highest form of spiritual warfare, because when God answers, revival leads the church into powerful new advances in fulfilling the Great Commission."³

Many active participants in the prayer movement agree that God's highest desire is for us to reach the nations so that all the peoples of the earth can have the opportunity to join with us in worshiping, praising and glorifying Him. Certain kinds of prayer can be a big help in moving toward that goal.

PRAYER AND FASTING TO TEAR DOWN STRONGHOLDS

Dick Eastman of Every Home for Christ provides a graphic example of how strategic-level intercession can actually open not only individual hearts, but also an entire region, to effective evangelism. He tells how a pair of Every Home for Christ workers from the Solomon Islands set out to evangelize an unreached people group, the Kwaio, in a remote mountainous area of the Solomon Islands in the South Pacific. The missionaries knew it would not be easy. One government official and at least three other missionaries had previously been murdered by the Kwaio as they attempted to penetrate their territory. They were told by the coastal people on the same island that if they dared go into those mountains they would certainly lose their lives.

The workers were not unwilling to risk their lives, but neither did they want to be foolish. They clearly understood what many Western missionaries might have ignored; namely, that the spiritual darkness of the region had been perpetrated by demonic forces—powerful territorial spirits—who had been doing just as they wished to the Kwaio for centuries. They also knew that the only way to break such power was through strategic-level intercession. Their first step, therefore, was to spend seven days in prayer and fasting.

Dick Eastman reports, "As the seven days unfolded, supernatural insights flowed into the hearts of the praying workers. Discernment and knowledge came regarding a host of demonic spirits and principalities controlling the region. Strange-sounding names were revealed in prayer, and as each was identified the workers would pray fervently until a sense of victory came. One of the leaders kept count of these confrontations, and before the seven days had passed, eighty-seven 'strongholds' had been identified and dealt with in prayer. Only then did the workers feel spiritually prepared to move into those treacherous mountains."[4]

The missionaries then walked into the forbidden territory and were allowed to enter the Kwaio village unharmed. For several hours they sat and talked to a group of village elders who were protecting their chief. The chief was a powerful witch doctor who was too ill to see them, but the workers knew that without the chief's permission nothing would happen. Every request to visit the chief was refused, but the Christian workers persisted. Finally the Holy Spirit broke the resistance and the two evangelists were allowed to visit him. Surprisingly enough, the chief listened attentively to the message, and opened his heart to accept Jesus Christ. No sooner did he do this, then he dropped dead!

The immediate reaction of the tribespeople was that these strangers had come and cursed their chief with their strange religion! They began making plans to execute them, but for two hours the Holy Spirit postponed their action by orchestrating a vigorous dialogue. Finally, the workers were freed. Then, amazingly, some seven hours later, the chief sat up, and called for his family and his friends to come to him. He explained how what must have been an angel had just taken him to a place where multitudes were worshiping the "Jesus," whom the missionaries had preached. Although he knew nothing of the Bible, he said he had been introduced to a person named "Abraham" and another named "Elijah." After many other remarkable details, he sent to have the missionaries returned to the village and begged his people to believe their message. Then the next day, he lay back down and calmly went to sleep forever to be with Jesus.

Not surprisingly, every Kwaio present immediately prayed to receive Jesus. By the time Eastman filed his report, some three years later, the resulting church in the chief's village had more than 300 converts, and throughout that mountainous region more than 16 other churches were in one stage of development or another. More than 4,000 Kwaio had by then given their lives to Jesus Christ![5]

"HOW COULD SUCH A THING HAPPEN?"

Many, moved by this dramatic story, will naturally ask, "How could such a thing happen?" Let's analyze it a bit.

- The workers' (Pacific Islanders) worldview allowed them to understand that the powers of the invisible world, both powers of darkness and powers of light, greatly influence what happens here in the visible world. They also knew that the invisible God was supreme and that He could and would intervene in human affairs by performing miraculous acts.
- They understood that prayer, both two-way prayer (chapter 2) and strategic-level intercession (this chapter) were essential for penetrating the powers of darkness over the Kwaio.
- They, through prayer, accomplished a form of "spiritual mapping," which revealed to them even the names of the spirits of darkness that held the Kwaio in bondage. I will explain spiritual mapping in the next chapter.
- Acting on the information they had, they "bound the

strongmen" and thereby "tore down the strongholds" that had been blocking the gospel from penetrating their region. These two things should be understood in some more detail.

Not too long ago, I relegated the term I heard from time to time, "binding the strongman," to the lunatic fringe. Those who were using it undoubtedly knew something of the Bible and of the work of the Holy Spirit in the world today that I had never been taught.

"BINDING THE STRONGMAN"?

I can remember, not too long ago, when I relegated the term I heard from time to time, "binding the strongman," to the lunatic fringe. I now realize that those who were using it, mostly Pentecostals and charismatics at that time, undoubtedly knew something of the Bible and of the work of the Holy Spirit in the world today that I had never been taught.

As a professor of church growth, one of my favorite Bible verses has long been Jesus' words to Peter and the disciples in Matthew 16: "On this rock I will build My church" (v. 18). This is the first time it is recorded that Jesus ever mentioned the word "church," and "building." It is another way of saying "growing" it. That was the part of the verse I stressed for the years I knew virtually nothing about strategic-level spiritual warfare. Jesus went on to say, "and the gates of Hades shall not prevail against it." I should have known He was telling His disciples that building the Church would inevitably involve serious spiritual warfare, but even if I did, I would not have been able to explain what He might have meant.

I had a worse problem with the next verse, "And I will give you the keys of the kingdom of heaven, and whatever you bind on earth will be bound in heaven" (v. 19). Here was this "binding" again, something that, in my mind, Holy Rollers might talk about, but not well-balanced Christians like me. I now see how foolish I had been to miss the crucial point that the "keys of the kingdom" would open the "gates of Hades" so that they could no longer obstruct the growth of the Church throughout the world. What are those "keys"? Obviously something to do with "binding."

Jesus had already used the word "binding" (which is the Greek *deo*) in Matthew 12 when He was teaching His disciples spiritual warfare. He said, "How can one enter a strong man's house and plunder his goods, unless he first binds the strong man?" (v. 29). In the parallel passage found in Luke 11, Luke uses the word "overcome" (which is the Greek *nikao*) the strongman (v. 22). The point I am making is that, biblically speaking, "binding" the strongman and "overcoming" the strongman are synonyms.

OVERCOMERS GET REWARDS

I wish I had known that sooner because, for some reason, "overcoming" seemed like a more respectable word than "binding" to me. Especially in the seven epistles Jesus wrote (through the pen of the apostle John) to the seven churches in Asia Minor in Revelation 2 and 3, the word "overcome" is repeated again and again. It is the only command kind of verb to appear in all seven of the epistles (except for the tag line "he who has an ear, let him hear what the Spirit says to the churches"). Furthermore, each time it appears, Jesus offers a lavish promise to whoever overcomes, such as, "To him who overcomes I will grant to sit with Me on My throne" (Rev. 3:21). From the first time I read the book of Revelation, I wanted to be an overcomer!

Besides using this word *nikao* seven times in Revelation, Jesus uses it only twice more in the whole Bible. Once it refers to what He does, and once it refers to what His disciples are supposed to do. The first is John 16:33: "Be of good cheer, I have overcome [*nikao*] the world." Jesus went on to climax this with His death on the cross where, Paul later says, "[He] disarmed principalities and powers, [and] He made a public spectacle of them, triumphing over them" (Col. 2:15). This is what Jesus did, laying the groundwork for all subsequent spiritual warfare. Is anything left for us to do?

Some like to think that because Jesus "overcame," we simply rest in Jesus and He will take care of all the power of evil for us. It is true that God is the only one who has the ultimate power over evil spirits, but He also has chosen to allow us to play a role in releasing that power. Jesus gave the word for believers to "overcome" in Revelation, long after His death and resurrection. Jesus' only further use of the word, besides John 16:33, is in Luke 11:22 where He is teaching His disciples that they must overcome or bind the strongman. Let's look at this passage more closely.

BREAKING THE GRIP OF BEELZEBUB

The Pharisees had accused Jesus of casting out demons by using the power of Beelzebub, the healing God of Ekron (see 2 Kings 1:2,3,6,16), a demonic spirit still worshiped during Jesus' time. Jesus, however, said no, He had cast them out by using the "finger of God" (Luke 11:20), who is the Holy Spirit. Here Beelzebub is revealed as a high-ranking demonic principality (see Matt. 12:24,27; Mark 3:22; Luke 11:15,18), just under Satan (see Matt. 12:26; Mark 3:23,26; Luke 11:18). He is called "the ruler of demons," and is like a general in the army who would be a ruler of soldiers, Satan himself being the commander in chief. Beelzebub is one of the strongmen of the kingdom of evil. So Jesus says, "When a strong man, fully armed, guards his own palace, his goods are in peace" (Luke 11:21). Obviously, the most precious goods of a demonic principality are unsaved souls. If his armor remains intact, apparently the unsaved souls he possesses remain unsaved. He gets his way!

The armor of the strongman, though, can be taken away when "a stronger than he comes upon him and overcomes him" (v. 22). The "stronger one" is the Holy Spirit, the finger of God. Where is the Holy Spirit today? He is in us! Jesus said, "You shall receive power when the Holy Spirit has come upon you" (Acts 1:8). Without the Holy Spirit, Jesus would not have commanded us to "overcome," but with the power of the Holy Spirit, Jesus said, "the works that I do he will do also" (John 14:12). This is why it is our duty to "bind the strongman." "Whatever you bind on earth will be bound in heaven" (Matt. 16:19).

During their seven days of prayer and fasting, the Every Home For Christ workers in the Solomon Islands were proactively binding the strongmen whose precious goods were the Kwaio people. Through strategic-level intercession, they took away their demonic armor and released the captives so that, for the first time, the Kwaio could hear the gospel of Christ.

PULLING DOWN STRONGHOLDS

I like the way Dick Eastman comments that through this strategic-level intercession, according to the records they kept, the two missionaries to the Kwaio people, "eighty-seven 'strongholds' had been identified and dealt with in prayer."[6] This is a reference to 2 Corinthians 10:4, where Paul says, "For the weapons of our warfare are not carnal but mighty in God for pulling down strongholds." Paul goes on to mention that "strongholds" take on two different forms: (1) "arguments" (Greek *logizomai*) and (2) "high things" (Greek *hypsoma*) (2 Cor. 10:5).

Many are ambiguous or inaccurate in their understanding of the nature of strongholds because they fail to recognize the two different forms. "Arguments" are strongholds rooted in human mind-sets or decisions or choices, whether by individuals or by groups such as national governments. When, for example, the United States government chooses to break a solemn treaty it previously signed with the Sioux, it immediately creates a stronghold the enemy can use until it is pulled down. I elaborate on this in chapter 5: "The Power to Heal the Past."

"High things" are spiritual principalities such as, for example, territorial spirits. They do not originate in human mind-sets, but in the invisible world of darkness. *The New International Dictionary of New Testament Theology* says, "The New Testament use of *hypsoma* probably reflects astrological ideas and hence denotes cosmic powers,...powers directed against God, seeking to intervene between God and [humans]."[7] The Every Home for Christ workers successfully neutralized 87 "high things" or demonic strongholds in the Solomon Islands through seven days of strategic-level intercession.

SHARING CHRIST IS A MUST

It would be easy to conclude that all we need to do is pray correctly and people will ipso facto get saved. As a matter of fact, this does happen from time to time. We do hear of people being saved through divine intervention, as the apostle Paul was on the Damascus road. It is not the usual way, though. The Bible says, "How then shall they call on Him in whom they have not believed? And how shall they believe in Him of whom they have not heard? And how shall they hear without a preacher?" (Rom. 10:14).

Let's be clear: "Binding the strongman" or "pulling down strongholds" never, by themselves, have saved a soul. Lost people are saved only through personal faith in Jesus Christ as Lord and Savior. Many people in your neighborhood and around the world, however, are not in positions to *hear* the gospel, no matter how brilliantly it is presented to them, because "the god of this age" has "blinded their minds," according to 2 Corinthians 4:4. Strategic-level intercession is simply a means God has entrusted to us to remove the blinders and loose the captives so they can finally hear the gospel. Then, they must decide whether they will commit their lives to Jesus Christ.

Many Kwaio were saved, but not all. The rest need continued and persistent aggressive evangelism because God is not willing that any of them should perish. A greater harvest is now a distinct possibility, however, because God's people engaged in powerful prayer.

■ REFLECTION QUESTIONS ■

1. The Brazilian missionary came up against the alleged "Prince of Peru." What do you think are the chances of a "Prince of the United States"? or "Prince of Wyoming"? or Prince of Houston"?
2. Why is it that most Americans scoff at the idea of demonic spirits controlling certain territories, while most Africans agree with it?
3. Have you yourself prayed or have you heard others pray to "bind the strongman" or to "bind Satan"? Discuss what this means.
4. Review the difference between the two kinds of strongholds, "arguments" and "high things," then try to give examples of each.

Notes
1. This report, received from Thomas Moreno and Dawn Ministries, was published in Steve Bufton's "Friday Fax," March 18, 1996.

2. Evelyn Christenson, *A Time to Pray* (Eugene, Oreg.: Harvest House Publishers, 1996), p. 50.
3. David Bryant in personal correspondence with the author.
4. Dick Eastman, *The Jericho Hour* (Orlando, Fla.: Creation House, 1994), p. 47.
5. This case study was paraphrased from Dick Eastman's book *The Jericho Hour,* pp. 43-47. It is retold, in greater detail, in Eastman's more recent book *Beyond Imagination* (Grand Rapids: Chosen Books, 1997), pp. 221-230.
6. Ibid., p. 47.
7. J. Blunck, "Height," *The New International Dictionary of New Testament Theology,* Vol. 2, ed. Colin Brown (Grand Rapids: Zondervan Publishing House, 1975), p. 200. See also *Theological Dictionary of the New Testament,* Vol. 8, ed. Gerhard Friedrich (Grand Rapids: Wm. B. Eerdmans Publishing Company, 1972), pp. 613-614.

FURTHER RESOURCES

- *Warfare Prayer* (1992) and *Confronting the Powers* (1996) by C. Peter Wagner (Ventura, Calif.: Regal Books). *Warfare Prayer* is the first book in *The Prayer Warrior Series,* providing an overview of the theory and practice of strategic-level intercession. *Confronting the Powers* is my more recent response to several criticisms raised against strategic-level intercession.

- *Possessing the Gates of the Enemy* by Cindy Jacobs (Grand Rapids: Baker Books, 1991; revised edition, 1994). This is an outstanding how-to book for those desiring to become active in strategic-level intercession.

- *The Jericho Hour* by Dick Eastman (Orlando, Fla.: Creation House, 1994). How powerful prayer is tearing down strongholds in many parts of the world.

- *The Handbook for Spiritual Warfare* by Ed Murphy (Nashville: Thomas Nelson Publishers, 1992). This is the most exhaustive textbook about spiritual warfare available, and contains strong biblical content.

- *Spiritual Warfare for Every Christian* by Dean Sherman (Seattle, Wash.: YWAM Publishing, 1990). An excellent, basic introduction to spiritual warfare containing a special emphasis on the personal life of the warrior.

Targeting Our Prayers: Spiritual Mapping

I N THIS DAY AND AGE, IT WOULD BE HARD TO IMAGINE BEING wheeled into an operating room for surgery when all the surgeon had to go on was an external diagnosis, no X rays or magnetic resonance imaging (MRI)s. A few generations ago, of course, this was the only way it could be done, and surgeons could be pardoned for mistakes made for lack of precise information. No longer can this be the case! A surgeon nowadays who does not use the latest technology to indicate ahead of time precisely where and how to cut would likely face a malpractice lawsuit if anything happened to go wrong.

X RAYS AND SMART BOMBS

Harold Caballeros, a Guatemalan pastor, says, "What an X ray is to a physician, spiritual mapping is to intercessors."[1]

I can hardly imagine a more vivid analogy. This chapter will help us understand, first of all, why spiritual mapping is important and second, how to begin doing it the proper way.

I also like the way Pastor Bob Beckett describes it. He takes us back to the Persian Gulf War when Saddam Hussein launched many Scud missiles, but which did minimal damage to the Allied forces. Someone satirically suggested that after he shot off his missiles, Hussein would tune to CNN television to find out where they had hit! Beckett admits this is the way his church, The Dwelling Place, in Hemet, California, prayed for years. He says, "We were striking out at the enemy but because of our lack of strategic information, we were incapable of isolating or discerning a specific target, aiming at it and hitting it."[2]

Beckett contrasts the Scud missiles with the "smart bombs" of the allies. As we saw on our television screens, they would enter right into the smokestack or window or door of the place at which they were aimed. The reason they could do this was that before the air war began, a small number of skillful reconnaissance specialists went behind enemy lines, located the high priority targets and programmed the targeting coordinates into the computers on the smart bombs.

As I have heard Bob Beckett say many times: "We have had all too much Scud missile praying in our churches. We need more smart bomb praying!"

WHY SOME PRAYERS ARE UNANSWERED

Follow with me in this series of five hypothetical questions, all of which have predictable answers.

> Does your church pray? The answer, of course, is yes.
> I have yet to find a church that does not pray.
> Does your church pray for individuals? Yes.
> Does your church pray for families? Yes.

Does your church pray for the pastor and the church?
Yes.
Does your church pray for your community? Yes.

I would further imagine that if I came to your church on a given Sunday morning and said to the congregation, "Let's spend the next 10 minutes in hearing testimonies of answered prayer for individuals here in the church," filling the time would be no problem. The same would go for answered prayers for families, and prayers for the pastor and the church. If I asked for answered prayers for the *community,* however, most churches would have a hard time filling even 2 minutes, never mind 10. Many would have to admit they have been praying for their community for 10 years and it is worse now than it was 10 years ago.

Why is this? It is so common that almost anyone reading this book can identify with what I have said. The same people are praying. They have the same theology of prayer. They have the same Holy Spirit. They are praying to the same heavenly Father. Why, then, do they ordinarily see more specific answers to their prayers for individuals, families and the church than they see to prayers for the community? I believe the answer is simple.

Suppose a person walks up to me, which people frequently do, and says, "Peter, would you please pray for me?"

Of course, I agree to pray for the person, but what is the first thing I do? I don't just start to pray. I say, "What would you like me to pray for?"

Suppose the person says, "I don't feel well right now."

I am still not ready to pray. I say, "Can you tell me what's wrong?" Up till this point, I do not know whether I am supposed to be praying about a sinus condition or the threat of losing a job or breaking up with a girlfriend, or what. So I keep asking questions until I have enough information. Only then do I start to pray for the person. You would do the same thing.

CAN WE TALK TO OUR COMMUNITY?

Why do we go through this routine? Obviously, it is because long ago we have learned through experience that the more specifically we pray for an *individual* the more likely we are to see our prayers answered. Our problem is that most of us have never learned how to ask such direct questions of our *community*. It has hardly ever even occurred to us that we should be doing such a thing.

The title of chapter 1 is "Prayer Can Be Powerful (Or Otherwise)." The rest of this book has been written to help all of us pray in the most powerful way possible. Spiritual mapping, or targeting our prayers as accurately as we can, is one of the more important helps we can use to pray powerfully instead of otherwise.

Let me give you an example. Just a few days ago, I read a report from Sri Lanka in the *Foursquare World Advance* magazine. It told how a Pastor Kumarawansa and his family entered an area of Sri Lanka called Horona and started a church in a house. They did warfare prayer against the territorial spirits of the area in their customary way. They had been well trained in strategic-level intercession. Still, little happened. They experienced great resistance to the gospel. Groups of unbelievers came and stoned the house where they were worshiping, disrupting the meetings.

Things were looking bleak, until one day a woman from Horona came to Mrs. Kumarawansa and gave her the name of the leading spirit over the area. Finally, they had the target they needed. They immediately switched from "Scud missile praying" to "smart bomb praying" against the specific ruling demonic principality. In the name of Jesus of Nazareth and by the power of the Holy Spirit, they took authority over demon so-and-so. The spiritual atmosphere cleared and things began to change rapidly. The report says, "The congregation is growing and a central church is anticipated from which ministry will flow to the entire region."[3]

What obviously made the difference in Horona was spiritual mapping. In this case, the intercessors played a passive role except for beseeching God to show them the solution to the problem of evangelistic blockage. God gave them the target coordinates for their prayers through the visit of the woman to the pastor's wife. God does this from time to time, but He also has given us many tools we can use to move into our communities and engage in more intentional, proactive and aggressive spiritual mapping. We now know a good bit about how to ask significant questions of our communities so that intercessors can target their prayers more accurately.

DEFINING "SPIRITUAL MAPPING"

The term "spiritual mapping" was coined by George Otis Jr., of The Sentinel Group, back in 1990. His desire is to help us "learn to see the world as it really is, not as it appears to be."[4] George Otis has become what I like to call "our number one Christian espionage agent." His books *The Last of the Giants* (Chosen Books) and *The Twilight Labyrinth* (Chosen Books) have revealed many of his findings, and more books are coming.

The implications of Otis's statement, simple as it may sound, are vast. For one thing, it presupposes that an invisible world exists out there somewhere beyond the visible world to which we relate with our five senses day in and day out. Second, it implies that some things about the invisible world may be more important to understand than some things in the visible world. This should not surprise us if we remember that the apostle Paul says, "We do not look at the things which are seen, but at the things which are not seen. For the things which are seen are temporary, but the things which are not seen are eternal" (2 Cor. 4:18).

It is remarkable that up until recently we as the Body of Christ have been ignorant of the invisible world. Oh, we have known about heaven and hell and God and the devil, and many of us have been casting out demons. That, however, is not enough to wage an effective war.

George Otis says, "One would think the ways of the spiritual dimension would be as familiar to the average believer as the sea is to mariners."[5] Such, however, is far from the case. Why? Otis goes on to say, "The problem seems to be that many believers—particularly in the Western hemisphere—have not taken the time to learn the language, principles and protocols of the spiritual dimension."[6] He might have added that we have not had many teachers. In the years I spent in graduate schools of theology and religion, I was not told such knowledge existed. I had no idea it was possible, as Otis says, to "[superimpose] our understanding of forces and events in the spiritual domain onto places and circumstances in the material world."[7]

WARRIORS VALUE INFORMATION ABOUT THE ENEMY

No one should question whether collecting information about the enemy ahead of time is biblical. God Himself said to Moses, "Send men to spy out the land of Canaan, which I am giving to the children of Israel" (Num. 13:2). Moses wanted to know how many people lived there, an estimate of their strength, what their cities were like, how they grew crops and whether the land included forests (vv. 18-20). He knew the value of detailed information. Joshua, one of the 12 who went to spy, later sent 2 spies into Jericho to bring him a more specific and up-to-date report before he would cross the Jordan River to take possession of the Promised Land.

Our battle today may not be like that of Joshua, who had to fight human beings in the visible world. Paul says, "We do not wrestle against flesh and blood, but against principalities, against powers, against the rulers of the darkness of this age, against spiritual hosts of wickedness in the heavenly places"

(Eph. 6:12). The principle, however, is the same whether we are interacting with the visible world or the invisible world: We gather all the intelligence we can before we move out to engage the enemy.

It is foolish to decide not to plan in advance. Paul writes, "lest Satan should take advantage of us;...we are not ignorant of his devices" (2 Cor. 2:11). Let's turn this around for just a moment. Suppose that somehow we *are* ignorant of Satan's devices. What will happen? Why, of course, *he will take advantage of us.* I like the way Ed Silvoso says it: "In active warfare, the most critical information is not what you know, but what you *don't* know. Especially if your enemy knows that you don't know it."[8]

I am afraid that Satan has been getting away with far too much these days. We have been woefully ignorant of what he and his hosts of wickedness have been up to in our cities, in our nations and around the world.

Silvoso agrees: "Generally speaking, the Church today is dangerously ignorant of the schemes of the devil. In fact, some people make it a point of pride *not* to know much about the devil and his devices. They haughtily declare that they will focus exclusively on Jesus and forget the devil."[9] Those days are rapidly coming to a close, though. People such as George Otis Jr., and escalating numbers of equally consecrated and skillful spiritual mappers cause Satan, more than ever before, to generate "great wrath, because he knows that he has a short time" (Rev. 12:12).

DO WE GLORIFY SATAN?

Does gathering large amounts of information about Satan and the demonic world of darkness tend to glorify Satan? A few leaders have been waving red flags and saying we should not probe too deeply into what has been happening in the invisible world. They suggest we should look only to Jesus, "the author and finisher of our faith" (Heb. 12:2).

In response, I must say I have never heard a spiritual mapper argue against looking to Jesus. I must also say if looking to Jesus means remaining ignorant of the devices of Satan, it is not what the author of Hebrews could have had in mind. Joshua did not gather information about the Canaanites in Jericho to glorify the Canaanites, but to defeat them.

Few would argue that medical research tends to glorify the disease. There was a time, for example, when smallpox was killing more people than AIDS is killing today. We applauded scientists who spent years in learning everything they could about smallpox and then breathed a sigh of relief when they finally developed a vaccine. I do not believe that as they were working anyone at all suggested they should do less for fear of glorifying smallpox. We are confronting a much worse enemy who has power to steal, to kill and to destroy. The obvious purpose of spiritual mapping is not to glorify such things, but rather to destroy them.

SPIRITS CAN BE TERRITORIAL

From time to time I have used the term "territorial spirits." This is not to imply that every demon is confined to a limited geographical arena, but it is to imply that some, perhaps many, might well be. The knowledge we have about the mobility patterns of the forces of darkness is admittedly limited. We get certain ideas about them from Frank Peretti's novels, but Peretti himself will be the first to remind us that he is writing fiction and the degree to which it coincides with fact is a subject for further research. Fortunately, the necessary research is well underway, led, as I have said, by George Otis Jr.

Otis says, "Nested near the heart of spiritual mapping philosophy is the concept of territorial strongholds....As anyone who has paid more than a casual visit to places such as India, Navajoland, Cameroon, Haiti, Japan, Morocco, Peru, Nepal, New Guinea and China will attest, elaborate hierarchies of deities and spirits are regarded as commonplace. These incorporeal beings are perceived to rule over homes, villages, cities, valleys, provinces and nations, and they exercise extraordinary power over the behavior of local peoples."[10]

Some high-ranking spirits are assigned certain territories and they have the ability to postpone the accomplishment of certain things God has willed.

One of the biblical windows through which God has allowed us a glimpse of the invisible world, fleeting as it might be, is Daniel 10. The chapter does not provide a method for conducting spiritual warfare, much less for undertaking spiritual mapping research. It does, however, provide two pieces of information that help us greatly in understanding what we are facing: (1) some high-ranking spirits are assigned certain territories and (2) they have the ability to postpone the accomplishment of certain things God has willed. Let's take a look.

Daniel had received a vision that caused him to begin an extended season of prayer and fasting. On the first day of his fast, God sent an angel to minister to Daniel. The angel, however, could not get straight through to the prophet. Why? When he arrived, he said to Daniel, "The prince of the kingdom of Persia withstood me twenty-one days; and behold, Michael, one of the chief princes, came to help me" (v. 13). Then, just before he left, he said, "And now I must return to fight with the prince of Persia; and when I have gone forth, indeed the prince of Greece will come" (v. 20).

Many other principles and teachings and lessons can be derived from this story, but, as a minimum, we learn that some spirits, which have considerable power, bear names such as the "Prince of Persia" and the "Prince of Greece," clearly territorial designations. It sounds a great deal like the "Prince of Peru" mentioned in chapter three of this book.

This makes sense when we begin to ask questions concerning the devil's modus operandi. One of his chief desires, as we have previously seen, is to blind the minds of unbelievers against hearing the gospel (see 2 Cor. 4:3,4). Satan is not God, though, and therefore he does not have the attributes of God. Satan, for example, is not omnipresent, as God is. Because he is a creature rather than the Creator, Satan can be in only one place at one time. Still, at this writing he has succeeded in blinding the minds of about 3 billion lost souls around the world. How does he accomplish this? He cannot be in 3 billion places at once.

Obviously, Satan must delegate the responsibility of blinding minds to myriad spiritual beings at his disposition in the invisible kingdom of darkness. The only place he sends these spirits is where there are people, and it would be logical to assume that the more people, the more quantity and quality (in the negative sense) of spirits would be expected.

Wherever human beings group themselves together, such as in neighborhoods, in cities, in regions or in nations, it could be expected that higher-ranking spirits, who have many others under their command, would be assigned. They are the ones we sometimes refer to as "territorial spirits." Where people develop a group affinity such as religious allegiance or vocation or some voluntary associations, however, the spirits over them might not be so confined to a geographical territory. For example, I would not be surprised if certain principalities were assigned to industries such as the meat-packing industry or the gold-mining industry or the automobile industry and so on.

NAMING THE SPIRITS?

Those who regularly minister in ground-level spiritual warfare know that demons are personalities and that they have names. Sometimes their names are functional, such as "spirit of lust" or "spirit of rejection." Sometimes they are proper names such as "Legion" (Mark 5:9). In the process of delivering an individual from demons, particularly in some of the more difficult cases, those who are ministering frequently experience a major break-through almost the moment they discover the name of the demon.

This is not to say that naming the spirits is a prerequisite for personal deliverance. I have seen success at times through saying, "Unclean spirit, whoever you may be, get out!" At other times, however, we ask for the name. For example, in his excellent book *Defeating Dark Angels,* Charles Kraft says, "If I don't have an idea of what the spirit's name might be, I command it to tell me what it is. Getting them to admit their names is often difficult."[11] The reason for this is that the spirits know they are more vulnerable if their names are known. They then become the bull's-eye in the center of the target.

Let's go back to Cindy Jacobs's insight that praying to free nations from the bondage of evil is much like praying to free individuals. I think the principle of knowing the name carries over from ground-level spiritual warfare to strategic-level spiritual warfare. It is not necessary that the name be known, but it can help greatly in certain circumstances.

To review briefly what we saw in chapter 1, when Paul was in Philippi, one of the greatest obstacles to spreading the gospel was a demonic power in a slave girl referred to in our

English translations as a "spirit of divination" (Acts 16:16). That would be its *functional* name, but in this case a literal translation of the original Greek would give us its *proper* name, "Python." Paul cast out the spirit, which I think could well have been the major territorial spirit over the city, and as a result he planted a strong, growing church.

Earlier in this chapter, I reported the incident in Sri Lanka in which the prayers of the church planters seemed to be ineffective until someone told the pastor's wife the name of the territorial spirit over the city. That was the key to breaking its power and allowing the gospel to spread. We will also recall from the first chapter that Thomas Muthee of the Kenya Prayer Cave discovered that the name of the principality over Kiambu was "Witchcraft," and that the spirit's chief human channel was "Momma Jane." Knowing this helped greatly in evangelizing the city, according to Pastor Muthee.

The experience of Harold Caballeros of Guatemala is similar to that of Thomas Muthee in Africa. Caballeros says, "We have learned that it is to our advantage to know who the strongman is in order to bind him and divide his spoils. Spiritual mapping helps us identify the strongman. In some cases, spiritual mapping will give us a series of characteristics that will guide us directly to the territorial prince or power. In other cases, we will find ourselves facing a natural person whom Satan is using. In still others, we will find ourselves face-to-face with a corrupt social structure."[12] The confrontation with evil can take shape in a variety of ways.

Although I have received more criticism for bringing to attention this matter of knowing the names of the spirits than I would ordinarily have expected, it should not seem odd. The prestigious *New International Dictionary of New Testament Theology* states: "In the faith and thought of virtually every nation the name is inextricably bound up with the person, whether of a man, a god, or a demon. *Anyone who knows the name of a being can exert power over it"* (italics mine).[13] This seems to be the consensus among scholars and those people, Christians or not, who have a better than average working knowledge of the invisible world.

Therefore, part of our process of spiritual mapping is to discover, if and when it is possible, the names of the principalities and powers that appear to be the major obstacles to evange-

---

The more we can target our prayers to God for pulling down strongholds, the more powerful our prayers are likely to be.

---

lism. When we do, we can then bind them specifically, and not just attempt to bind a supposed strongman in some general sense. Not that the latter is totally ineffective, but we are also learning that the more we can target our prayers to God for pulling down strongholds, the more powerful our prayers are likely to be.

THE THREE CRUCIAL QUESTIONS

Spiritual mapping, in some cases, can be a complex and sophisticated procedure. For example, to research the information about the devices Satan is currently using to obstruct spreading the gospel, which are found in his remarkable new book *The Twilight Labyrinth*, George Otis Jr. spent several years and hundreds of thousands of dollars in many nations of the world. Few people in a given generation of Christians would be called upon to do spiritual mapping on that level, although we are grateful to God for the select few He has chosen to do it.

At the same time, God is calling increasing numbers of ordinary Christians to begin to pray fervently and regularly for their own neighborhoods or towns or cities. Those who desire that their prayers be as effective as possible can also launch out in much more simplified spiritual mapping projects. Almost anyone who so desires can do *some* spiritual mapping. In undertaking any spiritual mapping project, whether large or small, whether complex or simplified, it is good to keep in mind three crucial questions that will help you maintain the overall focus:

1. *What is wrong with the community?* Of course, if nothing is wrong with your community, it is unnecessary to do either spiritual mapping or aggressive intercession. Few people, however, could conclude that nothing is wrong. The list of what is wrong at times is so long that it is difficult to sort out or prioritize which issues to tackle first.

2. *How did it get that way?* It may take some time to find the answers to this second question. Were the problems specified in question number 1 there since the founding of the city? Did they come in later? What was it that allowed them to begin? Many will make the mistake of starting to look for *natural* means to try to explain what is happening. George Otis Jr. warns against this and says, "Unfamiliar with the language, principles, and protocols of the spiritual dimension, they rely instead on political, economic, and cultural explanations for things. The problem here is a wrong assumption: namely that the material realm is the basement of reality. Unfortunately, wrong assumptions have a way of leading to wrong conclusions."[14]

3. *What can be done about it?* At this point, a transition is frequently made from the spiritual mapping *researchers* to the spiritual warfare *practitioners*. They

are not necessarily the same. Earlier in the chapter, we said that X rays are to the surgeon what spiritual mapping is to the intercessors. As all patients have noticed, when the X-ray technician finishes taking the pictures, no matter how anxious you are to know what the X rays might have shown about your malady, the technician will not inform you. Only the physician ordering the X rays is allowed to interpret them to the patient and decide on whatever treatment is necessary.

Some surgeons are not capable of operating the sophisticated X-ray equipment in their hospitals; they need the trained technicians. In the same way, intercessors need the patient,

In the Body of Christ, the eye needs the ear and the ear needs the hand. When we team up together, we can do wonderful things for God's kingdom that we could not do by ourselves.

spiritual mapping researchers. Those researchers, however, frequently are not gifted with the discernment necessary to understand the spiritual implications of all they have found, to say nothing about knowing how to go into the field and begin the spiritual battle. Some people, of course, combine the two, but we should not be surprised if they do not. In the Body of Christ, the eye needs the ear and the ear needs the hand. When we team up together, we can do wonderful things for God's kingdom that we could not do by ourselves.

THREE MAJOR AREAS FOR MAPPING

Significant pioneering work in spiritual mapping was done some years ago by the El Shaddai Church of Guatemala City under the leadership of Pastor Harold Caballeros. They undertook it, just as a reminder, not for the sake of exploring the domain of the devil, but to facilitate evangelizing their geographical area. The model they used is not necessarily a procedure that would be recommended for every person at every time. Many other approaches could work equally well. I do not want to conclude this chapter without at least one specific field example, though, and this approach is a particularly interesting and helpful one.

The El Shaddai Church divided its spiritual mapping team into three units, and the members of each unit were not allowed to communicate with each other during the process. Again, this is not a general principle; it is simply the way they chose to operate during this particular project. Each unit was assigned the task of researching the three major areas for spiritual mapping:

Historical factors. This group, using mainly library sources, researched the name of the community, why it got the name, the root meaning of the name and the possible relationship of the name to the spirit world or to false beliefs. They then examined the territory itself, explored its characteristics that distinguish it from surrounding places, the openness to the gospel, the churches, if any, the socioeconomic condition, the centers of iniquity in the community and changes that had recently taken place in the area. They also dug into the history of the region and asked questions about why it was founded, who the founders were, their religious roots, traumatic events of the past, the history of the church and suggestions of the presence of curses or territorial spirits.

Physical factors. Another unit studied material objects in and around the community. Caballeros observes, "It seems that the devil, due to his unlimited pride, frequently leaves a trail behind."[15] The beginning point of this research is studying maps, both old maps and new maps. Sometimes the layout of the city will suggest some kind of pattern. For example, a city laid out at 45° off true north and south raises suspicions of occult influence on the layout. This is often the case when the city is founded by Freemasons. Inventories are made of parks; monuments; archaeological sites; statues; centers of iniquity such as bars, abortion clinics, houses of prostitution or porno shops; centers of worship, both Christian and non-Christian; buildings that house centers of political, economic, judicial, educational, military or cultural power. The socioeconomic condition of each subarea of the community is also carefully observed.

Spiritual factors. A third unit checked the spiritual environment. This is a rather special team. Caballeros says, "Those called to work in this spiritual area are the intercessors, people who flow in the gift of discernment of spirits and accurately hear from God."[16] They will pray over the churches as well as over the occult and other non-Christian centers of worship, sense whether the heavens are open or closed, draw the internal spiritual boundaries between certain subareas and seek the identity of the specific principalities and powers who have evil power over the community.

After a period of intense work, the El Shaddai Church teams compared their notes and were amazed. The historical team had focused on a particular occult archaeological site dating back to the Mayan Empire. The physical factors team had located a vacant house right in the area that was a center of witchcraft. The spiritual factors team had discerned that the territorial spirit over the place was using a certain human practitioner of idolatry and witchcraft as the strongman. The intercessors mentioned certain physical characteristics this strongman had. They then began to do powerful strategic-level intercession directed toward those particular targets.

Practicing what I am calling "two-way prayer," at one point they heard clearly from God in one of those "quote-unquote" situations Jack Hayford describes (see chapter 2). The Lord said, "Tomorrow I will give you the man's first and last name in the newspaper on page so-and-so." To be sure, the next day the man's picture was on the designated page and he fit the physical description previously given to the intercessors. He turned out to be the owner of the vacant house right across the street from the Mayan archaeological site!

Using that information, a result of painstaking spiritual mapping, the prayers of the members of El Shaddai Church could become more targeted, and therefore more powerful, than they could have been otherwise. They believed their spiritual mapping project had opened more doors for advancing the gospel in their city than otherwise would be the case.

Because spiritual mapping is still in its infancy, we can collectively look forward to much more information and many more insights in the days to come. The more it progresses, the more powerful our prayers are likely to become.

Notes

1. Harold Caballeros, "Defeating the Enemy with the Help of Spiritual Mapping," *Breaking Strongholds in Your City*, ed. C. Peter Wagner (Ventura, Calif.: Regal Books, 1993), p. 125.
2. Bob Beckett, "Practical Steps Toward Community Deliverance," *Breaking Strongholds in Your City*, p. 158.
3. Anonymous, "Changed by the Power of God," *Foursquare World Advance* (September-October 1996): 5.
4. George Otis Jr., "An Overview of Spiritual Mapping," *Breaking Strongholds in Your City*, p. 32.
5. Ibid.
6. Ibid.
7. Ibid.
8. Ed Silvoso, *That None Should Perish* (Ventura, Calif.: Regal Books, 1994), p. 98.
9. Ibid., p. 100.
10. Otis, "An Overview of Spiritual Mapping," *Breaking Strongholds in Your City*, pp. 34, 35.
11. Charles H. Kraft, *Defeating Dark Angels* (Ann Arbor, Mich.: Servant Publications, 1992), p. 187.

12. Caballeros, "Defeating the Enemy with the Help of Spiritual Mapping," *Breaking Strongholds in Your City*, p. 136.
13. H. Beitenhard, "Name," *The New International Dictionary of New Testament Theology*, ed. Colin Brown, Vol. 2 (Grand Rapids: Zondervan Publishing House, 1976), p. 648.
14. George Otis Jr., *Spiritual Mapping Field Guide* (Lynnwood, Wash.: The Sentinel Group, 1993), p. 14.
15. Caballeros, "Defeating the Enemy with the Help of Spiritual Mapping," *Breaking Strongholds in Your City*, p. 141.
16. Ibid., p. 143.

■ REFLECTION QUESTIONS ■

1. If you started to raise spiritually significant questions about your community, what would two or three of the first ones be?
2. If we are in the midst of warfare, how important do you think it is to have accurate information about the enemy?
3. How would you respond to someone who says that if you do spiritual mapping you are glorifying Satan?
4. Discuss the differences between historical factors, physical factors and spiritual factors in spiritually mapping your city.

FURTHER RESOURCES

- *The Last of the Giants* (Grand Rapids: Chosen Books, 1991) and *The Twilight Labyrinth* by George Otis Jr. (Grand Rapids: Chosen Books, 1997). George Otis Jr. is the founder of the spiritual mapping movement, and therefore these two books are a must.
- *Spiritual Mapping Field Guide* by George Otis Jr., (Ventura, Calif.: Regal Books, 1997). This is a step-by-step instructional manual to be used by those who desire to undertake spiritual mapping projects.
- *Breaking Strongholds in Your City* edited by C. Peter Wagner (Ventura, Calif.: Regal Books, 1993). This is a

practical introduction to spiritual mapping and includes chapters by such experts as George Otis Jr., Harold Caballeros, Cindy Jacobs, Bob Beckett, C. Peter Wagner and others.

- For those desiring more information about ground-level spiritual warfare (casting out demons), here are the three books I recommend most: *Evicting Demonic Intruders* by Noel and Phyl Gibson (Chichester, England: New Wine Press, 1993); *Defeating Dark Angels* by Charles H. Kraft (Ann Arbor, Mich.: Servant Publications, 1992); *Deliverance from Evil Spirits* by Francis MacNutt (Grand Rapids: Chosen Books, 1995).

The Power to Heal the Past

THE DAYS IN WHICH WE LIVE ARE NOT NORMAL TIMES. WE are the first generation since Jesus' death at calvary that has the measurable potential of fulfilling Jesus' Great Commission. It may come as a surprise to some to learn that one reason no previous generation could say such a thing is simply that they did not possess the necessary tools to accurately measure either the progress of world evangelization to date or the remaining task. We now have the technology to do it, and the calculations are being carried out by our sophisticated Christian research centers.

LIGHT AT THE END OF THE GREAT COMMISSION TUNNEL

It is one thing to see light at the end of the Great Commission tunnel, but it is another actually to get the job done: namely, to establish a viable church-planting movement in every one of the yet unreached people groups of the world. When that is done, every baby born anyplace in the world, for the first time in history, will have a reasonable opportunity to hear the gospel of Jesus Christ in his or her lifetime. This is one way of saying that "this gospel of the kingdom will have been preached in all the world as a witness to all the nations," to paraphrase Jesus' words in Matthew 24:14.

For two thousand years, God's kingdom has steadily advanced through one "gate of Hades" after another, as Jesus would put it, reflecting His words in Matthew 16:18. As a result, Satan has his back to the wall, so to speak. George Otis Jr. says, "The soldiers of the Lord of hosts have now encircled the final strongholds of the serpent....While the remaining task is admittedly the most challenging phase of the battle, the armies of Lucifer are faced presently with a community of believers whose spiritual resources—if properly motivated, submitted and unified—are truly awesome."[1]

Why would Otis say we are faced with "the most challenging phase of the battle"? For at least two reasons.

First, it could be argued convincingly that the vast majority of the yet unreached people groups are located in that part of the world in which Satan has been more deeply entrenched for a longer period of time than he has in any other part of the world. The closer we get to the ancient sites of the Tower of Babel and the Garden of Eden, the truer this is likely to become.

The second reason is found in Revelation 12:12: "For the devil has come down to you, having great wrath, because he knows that he has a short time." If this is truly the generation that can complete the Great Commission, we should not be surprised if we are also those against whom Satan is unleashing unprecedented fury.

This is the reason world missions can no longer be a business-as-usual, status-quo operation. George Otis says, "Those

Christians who assume they can apply 1970s-vintage ministry strategies to 1990s realities are in for a rude awakening. Strategic plans and policy manuals written for yesterday's placid conditions are rapidly becoming museum pieces."[2]

AN EXTRAORDINARY POWER BOOST

Because world evangelization is a divine activity, executed through selected human agents, it is to be expected that God will supply His people with the knowledge, tools and resources necessary to complete the task. This is exactly what He seems to be doing in our days. I believe that God is now providing the greatest power boost to world missions we have seen since William Carey went to India 200 years ago to launch what we call "the modern missionary movement." This increased reservoir of power is being released through three extraordinarily powerful spiritual resources that are now available to the entire Body of Christ. Not that they are brand new, but in previous decades only a tiny segment of believers was in touch with them. The names of all three were coined after 1990. They are:

1. *Strategic-level spiritual warfare.* This is the subject of chapter 3.
2. *Spiritual mapping.* This is the subject of chapter 4.
3. *Identificational repentance.* This is the subject of this chapter.

So let's get on with it.

IDENTIFICATIONAL REPENTANCE

Isaiah 58:12 says, "Those from among you shall build the old waste places; you shall raise up the foundations of many generations; and you shall be called the Repairer of the Breach."

Apparently it is possible to go back and confront the wounds previous generations might have caused.

I have been a Christian and a church attender for almost 50 years, and I cannot recall ever hearing a sermon from the pulpit about identificational repentance or about healing the wounds of the past. I have four earned graduate degrees in religion from respectable academic institutions, and not one of my professors even hinted such a thing is possible. You cannot find sections about identificational repentance in the writings of classic theologians such as Martin Luther or John Calvin or John Wesley. That is why I say the topic of this chapter is "new." It is certainly new for many of us, but not new for the Scriptures, as we shall soon see.

We are extremely fortunate to have an outstanding new textbook about this subject called *Healing America's Wounds* by John Dawson (Regal Books). In my opinion, this is one of the most influential books of the decade for Christian leaders of all denominations. It is mainly because of the support Dawson's book provides that I now feel confident enough to write this chapter, my first extended writing about identificational repentance. I consider this so important that I require my Fuller Theological Seminary students to read *Healing America's Wounds* and I regularly invite John Dawson, who has founded the International Reconciliation Coalition, to come and help me teach my classes.

Since the publication of *Healing America's Wounds,* overt events for the express purpose of repentance and reconciliation have been rapidly escalating, not only in America, but in many other parts of the world as well. Japanese Christian leaders have gone to the cities of Asia to repent of Japanese occupation in World War II. Brazilian leaders have repented to Paraguayans for a brutal war that involved not only appropriating land that was not theirs, but a bloody massacre as well. Germans have gathered in Holland in repentance for atrocities of Hitler. New

Zealanders have publicly admitted and confessed their abuse and their oppression of the native Maori people.

Here in the United States, Lutherans have repented for the anti-Semitism found in Martin Luther's writings. Southern Baptists, at their national convention, took official action to apologize to African-Americans for endorsing slavery. Methodist leaders were among a group who repented on site of the sins of Col. John Chivington, a Methodist lay minister, who led the atrocious and shameful massacre of Arapaho and Cheyenne Indians at Sand Creek near Denver more than 100 years ago. Some months later, the United Methodist General Conference followed suit by passing a resolution denouncing their ancestors' actions and apologizing for the Sand Creek atrocity.

At a 1996 Promise Keepers rally of 50,000 in Washington, D.C.'s JFK Stadium, Pastor A. R. Bernard, an African-American, was one of the speakers. He spoke of the reality of generational sin. He argued that racism, passed from one generation to another, may well be the sin of the American nation that has most grieved the heart of God throughout our history. He called for repentance. He challenged white men to repent for their racism and he challenged minority men to repent for their bitterness. Thousands responded and gathered on the field in front of the platform, all of them deeply moved by the Holy Spirit and many of them openly weeping.

Any doubt of the sincerity and appropriateness of this act was convincingly dissolved by a remarkable celestial phenomenon. All day long the skies had been thickly overcast, some rain had been falling and the atmosphere had been a clammy 65 degrees. At about four o'clock in the afternoon the public repentance took place. The 50,000, some on the field and some in the stands, were singing together, "Stretch out Your hand and heal this nation." When they came to a line in the song, "Cause Your face to shine upon us again," the clouds instantly broke and the sun shone through for the first time that day. Within 10 minutes, not a cloud was left in the sky and the bright sunshine quickly raised the temperature in the stadium by five degrees, according to the thermometer on the scoreboard.[3]

These things, happening more and more frequently around the world, are clearly one of the more important things the Spirit is saying to the churches. Let's try to understand some of the principles behind this powerful spiritual tool God seems to be encouraging us to use. Let's have an ear to hear what the Spirit is saying to the churches.

PERSONAL REPENTANCE

Whereas "identificational repentance" might be an unfamiliar concept to many, "personal repentance" is not. Sin can and does invade our personal lives from time to time. When it does, not only does it affect us as individuals, but the ripple effect also can and often does move out to damage our families, our friends, our jobs, our health and our total quality of life. Can we do anything about this? Of course. This *is* something we have frequently heard preached from the pulpit. Every seminary student can pass an examination in the subject. We do find it repeatedly in the writings of Luther and Calvin and Wesley.

To review, we know that God loves us and desires to have fellowship with us. When sin enters our lives, however, it raises obstructions that prevent us from being all God wants us to be and it inhibits God from doing what he would otherwise seek to do in our lives. Our fellowship with our Father is no longer the same. It does not have to remain that way, though, because God has given us a chance to remit the sin that is at the root of whatever problems might have arisen.

A foundational principle is that "without shedding of blood there is no remission," as we read in Hebrews 9:22. Throughout the Old Testament, the blood shed for the remission of sins was ordinarily the blood of sacrificial bulls and goats and other animals. A new sacrifice was required for each new sin. Jesus, however, changed that once and for all when He shed His blood on the cross. The blood of Jesus is now sufficient to remit all sins wherever and whenever they might occur. We no longer sacrifice animals.

The necessary steps to secure remission of sins are familiar to all believers. We first identify the sin specifically. Generalities at this point will not suffice. It is not the time to waffle by saying, "Lord, if I might possibly have sinned..." or to confess some vague tendency toward sinning. Only if we call the sin we have

---

Americans' frontier spirit has instilled in us the notion that we are masters of our own destiny. We admire the "self-made man."

---

committed by its proper name can we move on to the next step, which is to confess the sin to God and ask His forgiveness. When we sincerely confess our sin, then God is "faithful and just to forgive us our sins and to cleanse us from all unrighteousness" (1 John 1:9). The sin is remitted. Our responsibility from that point on is to walk in obedience to God and then to repair whatever damage that sin might have caused others. In most cases, it is a fruitless effort to attempt to heal the wounds a given sin might have inflicted on others until the sin itself is confessed.

CONFRONTING *CORPORATE* SIN

As anthropologists frequently remind us, we Westerners in general and Americans in particular are characterized by an individualism that seems a bit strange to the majority of the human race. Our frontier spirit has instilled in us the notion that we are masters of our own destiny. We admire the "self-made man." We think we can pull ourselves up by our own bootstraps. If I am successful I expect to get the credit; if not, I expect to get the blame.

Other peoples of the world tend to think much more corporately. The decision of who a young person is to marry, for example, is ordinarily a group decision, not an individual choice. In many of the most significant cultures of the world, all important decisions are group decisions. Only unimportant matters are left to the individual's discretion.

I think this may be one of the reasons I have found that non-Western Christian leaders seem to have a much easier time grasping the concept of identificational repentance than some of us Westerners do. Identificational repentance is premised on the reality of corporate sin. In other words, not only do individuals sin, but *groups* of people also sin. This can be a group as small as a family (see Exod. 20:5,6; Lev. 18:25; Deut. 5:9) or as large as a nation (see Isa. 65:6,7; Jer. 11:10; 15:4,7; 16:10-12; Lam. 5:7). It can be a religious group, it can be a city, it can be a church, it can be an industry, it can be a government department, it can be a race or it can be a school.

Wherever many individuals are meaningfully linked together in a social network, that group can sin, not as individuals, but *as a group*. When it does, each individual member of the group is, to one degree or another, identified with the corporate sin whether the person personally participated in the act itself or not (see Exod. 32:9-14; Jer. 3:25; Ps. 106:6; Dan. 9:8,20; Ezra 9:6,7; Neh. 1:6,7; 9:2).

God gives us a way to confront corporate sin just as He gives us a way to confront individual sin. I believe that God has a purpose for every nation, whether a geopolitical nation or whether a culturally bonded people group. If that group sins corporately, however, the nation cannot be all that God wants it to be without the remission of the root sin. The classic Scripture for this is 2 Chronicles 7:14: "If My people who are called by My name will humble themselves, and pray and seek My face, and turn from their wicked ways, then I will hear from heaven, and will forgive their sin and heal their land." "Healing the land" obviously does not refer to the *individual* realm, but to the *corporate* realm. Therefore, "forgiving their sin," which is another way of talking about *remitting* their sin, means remitting *corporate* sin.

I like the way my friend Johannes Facius of the International Fellowship of Intercessors puts it. Facius says, "There is one major problem that stands in the way of healing the land. That is the unconfessed historical sins of the nation. Unconfessed sin is the foothold of satanic forces, whether we speak of the individual or of the nation. Unconfessed sin constitutes a basis for satanic rule. We must therefore find a way of dealing with it, if we are to see our people delivered from demonic strongholds."[4]

STEPS TOWARD REMITTING CORPORATE SIN

Our approach to remitting corporate sin is parallel to the way we handle individual sin.

First, we specifically identify the corporate sin or sins of the nation. This is a function of spiritual mapping, as I explained in the last chapter. For example, after years of careful study and analysis, I tend to agree with Dr. A. R. Bernard, the Promise Keepers speaker, who suggested that racism may be America's number one corporate sin. Some might mention abortion as a top candidate; but abortion, in my opinion, is a subset of racism because it is treating some human beings as if they did not really matter.

To be more specific and to get closer to the basement of reality, we soon see that one of the elemental strongholds allowing the enemy to perpetuate racism in our nation is, first of all, bringing Africans to our shores as slaves. I believe this is the number one corporate sin, in terms of magnitude, that our nation, as a nation, has committed. A deeper and more fundamental sin lies at the root of this, however: namely, the way we European immigrants to America treated our host people, the Native American nations. I think it is an arguable hypothesis that had we treated the Indians more justly, we may never have bought and sold African people as slaves. Canada, for example, treated what they call the "First Nations" differently and they never engaged in slave trade as we did.

A second step is to confess the national sin corporately and ask God for forgiveness. Because of the massive social implications of national sin, as contrasted to individual sin, this step ordinarily requires much more to achieve results. Rarely, if ever, can it be accomplished in only one public act. Going into great detail about what is required for adequate national repentance is complicated by the relative newness of this whole concept. Even those of us who are leaders in this movement find ourselves, at this writing, on a learning curve.

As an example, you may have noticed I said the Southern Baptists recently "apologized" for their participation in slavery. That has an identificational side to it, but some leaders who participated in the debate leading up to the decision argued that it would be inappropriate for those of us today to "repent" for the sins others had committed. I contend that it is highly appropriate, but I also realize it will take some longer than others to understand the biblical and theological principles behind identificational repentance. Further, I anticipate some will persist in their opposition and also criticize those of us who are advocates of identificational repentance.

The third step toward remitting corporate sin is to apply the blood of Jesus Christ and to ask God for forgiveness. Without the shedding of blood there is no remission of sin; but the blood of Jesus Christ cleanses us, corporately as well as individually, from all sin (see 1 John 1:7).

The final step is to walk in obedience and to do what is necessary to repair the damage caused by the sin. In many cases, this will become an extended process, particularly in those cases where the national iniquity has been passing through many generations. The reasons underlying this merit some explanation.

Iniquity Passes from Generation to Generation

My friend Gary Greig, associate professor of Old Testament at Regent University School of Divinity in Virginia Beach, Virginia, says, "The principle of generational sin—the cycling of sin, guilt, and bondage from generation to generation—reflects part of the essential holy character of the Lord." He refers to Exodus 20:5 and says, "[God's] holiness causes Him to visit or appoint the iniquity of parents upon their descendants to the third and fourth generation of those who hate him."[5]

It is helpful at this point to understand the difference between sin and iniquity. The sin is the specific act that was committed; the iniquity (*awon* in Hebrew) refers to the state of guilt resulting from that sin that is passed down through generations. We Americans, for example, suffer today from the corrupting effects of the iniquity of slavery in our society although none of us alive ever personally engaged in the slave trade itself. I believe that the phrase "third or fourth generation" can be understood as a figure of speech, meaning that it goes on and on. How long? Until the act of sin, which began the malignant process, is remitted by the shedding of blood.

Time does not heal the wound, but, instead, the wound becomes more and more painful as it moves to each succeeding generation. One biblical example is the sin of Cain murdering his brother, Abel. Five generations later, Lamech also committed murder and specifically identified his sin with that of his ancestor, Cain, by saying, "If Cain shall be avenged seven-fold, then Lamech seventy-sevenfold" (Gen. 4:24). Those of us who were in Los Angeles during the riots of 1972 are well aware that racism is not better than it was in previous genera-tions, but worse, despite a constant barrage of presidential admonitions, legislative actions and Supreme Court decisions. The prognosis is that it will continue to worsen until appropri-ate spiritual action is taken.

Only Christians Can Remit National Sins

Who can take the action to see that the causative sin is proper-ly repented of and forgiven by God? This takes us back to the principle that there is no remission of sin without the shedding of blood (see Heb. 9:22). The only blood now available for remitting sins is the blood of Jesus Christ. The only persons eli-gible to take the authority to repent and claim the power of Jesus' blood to forgive sins are those who have already been redeemed by His blood: namely, the Christians. Kings, prime ministers, chiefs, presidents, judges, generals or others, by virtue of their office and apart from Jesus' blood, cannot be designat-ed as the point persons for significant acts of repentance. They may, however, be present when such events occur and partici-pate in the public acts of acknowledging the repentance and offer whatever gestures of forgiveness may be appropriate.

It is worth reiterating that the Christians who take this ini-tiative to heal the wounds of the past may not be, and usually are not, among the generation that committed the root sin. They can, however, identify with that generation; but no one else can take on the burden of past sins. Certainly those who actually committed them cannot. They are dead and assigned their eternal destiny, whatever it may be. Let's not confuse iden-tificational repentance with resolving personal sins of any past individuals. We are not advocating, as some do, that living believers can be baptized for dead persons, nor are we suggesting that our actions can shorten sentences that some have received to spend time in purgatory.

Furthermore, in most cases honesty will reveal that the presence of the iniquity that has been passed through the generations is much more than symbolic. For example, as it became clearer and clearer to me that racism was the chief sin of my nation, I found myself moving out of years and years of denial that I myself could be infected with racism. Now I am finally able to admit that, although I never bought or sold a slave, I, too, am racist and I deeply regret it. When I participate in identificational repentance, therefore, I am not attempting to relieve myself of responsibility for the injustices I see around me. I make it a point to confess my own personal sin while I am also confessing the sins of my ancestors.

John Dawson summarizes it this way: "Unless somebody identifies themselves with corporate entities, such as the nation of our citizenship, or the subculture of our ancestors, the act of honest confession will never take place. This leaves us in a world of injury and offense in which no corporate sin is ever acknowledged, reconciliation never begins and old hatreds deepen."[6]

What does Dawson mean by "identification" in this context? He says that identification "signifies the act of consciously including oneself within an identifiable category of human beings."[7]

As examples, I can easily identify with the injustices perpetrated against Native Americans because my ancestors were among those who succeeded in creating conditions that drove the Mohawk Indians out of their native Mohawk Valley into Canada. I can also identify with the inhuman slavery industry simply because I am a white American.

CAN PAST SINS *REALLY* BE REMITTED?

It is difficult for some to accept the proposition that Christians in this generation can do anything at all about what happened in past generations. For example, one irate reader of *Charisma* magazine responded to an article about identificational repentance by writing these words: "I feel no obligation to apologize for the alleged faults of any great-great ancestor, nor do I expect to receive any apologies or recover any debts due that ancestor. If any Indians feel my ancestors injured their ancestors, then they can just ask my ancestors to apologize to their ancestors."[8]

Awhile ago I discussed the matter with a friend of mine who is a respected evangelical biblical scholar. He assured me that the notion of remitting sins of past generations is neither taught in the Bible, nor is it theologically sound. Many others would agree with my professor friend and with the *Charisma* reader.

One of the reasons for this, I think, is that our evangelical biblical orientation is heavily weighted to the New Testament, which has little to say about identificational repentance, either implicitly or explicitly. An abundance of New Testament teaching can be found about the corporate nature of sin and, to a lesser degree, the concept of identifying with the sins of peers. An abundance of Old Testament teaching can be found, however, about both corporate sin and the validity of living persons identifying with sins of those long gone from this earth.

For some reason, we frequently overlook the fact that the New Testament is based on the Old Testament. Gary Greig, who teaches Hebrew and Old Testament to seminary students, says, "Since the Old Testament was the Bible of the New Testament church [it] therefore offered the only scriptural model of sin and confession available to the early church."[9]

When Paul wrote to Timothy that "All Scripture is given by inspiration of God, and is profitable for doctrine, for reproof, for correction, for instruction in righteousness, that the man of God may be complete, thoroughly equipped for every good work" (2 Tim. 3:16-17), he was referring to the Old Testament, not to the Gospel of John or to 1 Peter or to the book of Acts.

If we agree that the apostles were "biblical" believers, we must realize that they knew and taught Old Testament principles.

I have already mentioned the corporate nature of 2 Chronicles 7:14, which affirms that God can and is disposed to forgive, or remit, the (corporate) sin of His people and heal their land. Some might argue that this may refer only to the sins of the contemporary generation, not to past generations. Nehemiah's prayer of confession, however, said, "*Both my father's house* and I have sinned" (Neh. 1:6, emphasis mine). Likewise, Daniel said, "I was...confessing my sin and *the sin of my people*" (Dan. 9:20, emphasis mine). In both these cases, Daniel and Nehemiah were identifying with and confessing sins of the idolatry of past generations that they themselves did not commit. At

---

If we agree that the apostles were "biblical" believers, we must realize that they knew and taught Old Testament principles.

---

the same time, they recognized they had been personally affected by the iniquity resulting from those sins.

REMITTING SAUL'S "ETHNIC CLEANSING"

David was the king when Israel once suffered a three-year famine. Believing in two-way prayer, he asked God if for any particular reason his people might be suffering what could soon become a life-and-death situation. God said, "It is because of Saul and his bloodthirsty house, because he killed the Gibeonites" (2 Sam. 21:1). Here is a case when the iniquity of the sin of a past generation actually was having a physical influence on a succeeding generation.

The Gibeonites, residents of the Promised Land, had succeeded in negotiating a covenant with Joshua so he would protect them and not liquidate them as he was doing to other groups occupying Canaan at the time (see Josh. 9). The Israelites had kept that covenant for 13 generations. We do not have the details of exactly how and why it happened, but at one point in time, King Saul, for some reason, apparently decided to do some "ethnic cleansing," and massacred many of the Gibeonites. This serious sin of breaking a solemn covenant was not properly handled by Saul's generation, but God had not forgotten it. The iniquity was passed on, and the judgment resulted in a famine.

David needed no further explanation. Well versed in the biblical principles of identificational repentance, he knew that the way out of the famine was to secure the remittance of the sin of Saul, a sin in which David did not participate at all as an individual. Saul could do nothing about it because he was dead and gone. As the king of Israel, it was David's responsibility to take corporate action on behalf of his nation.

Understanding that there is no remission of sin without the shedding of blood, the question then became: What blood should be shed? The unfolding story is one that has caused a good bit of discussion among biblical scholars because human sacrifice is forbidden by Jewish law (see Deut. 12:31). Questions arise whether David was at this point acting according to God's will, because what happened is strange. Nevertheless, David approached the surviving Gibeonites and asked them to decide exactly what blood should be shed.

David said, "With what shall I make atonement?" (2 Sam. 21:3). The Gibeonites responded that David should turn over to them seven blood descendants of Saul whom they would kill and then hang up their bodies for a public display. It goes without saying that since Jesus shed His blood, a call for such things is no longer necessary, but those days were different. David, rightly or wrongly, gave them the seven individuals, their blood was shed and the sin of King Saul in a past generation was forgiven.

The result? "And after that God heeded the prayer for the land" (v. 14). The famine ended!

I have found no clearer biblical teaching about healing the wounds of the past. The 12 apostles and other leaders of the Early Church knew the story of the atonement for the sins of Saul very well. The fact that they did not elaborate on identificational repentance in any of the Gospels or Epistles is no more significant, in my mind, than the fact that neither did they elaborate on the Old Testament use of musical instruments in worshiping God. Because of this, entire contemporary denominations have chosen to be "noninstrumental," but the collective wisdom of the Body of Christ through the ages has been otherwise.

For most of us, the fact that the Old Testament was the only Bible of the apostles leads us to assume that musical instruments were being used in the churches they planted and pastored. The same hermeneutical process could equally apply to the Old Testament assertion that, indeed, God desires to remit sins of past generations now in New Testament times.

RELEASING THE POWER OF IDENTIFICATIONAL REPENTANCE

This is a book about powerful prayer. Of all the forms of prayer I could list, none surpasses the potential of the prayer of identificational repentance for opening the way to spread the gospel. Why? Back in chapter 3, I stressed that the overriding reason unbelievers do not accept the Good News of Jesus Christ is that Satan, the god of this age, has succeeded in blinding their minds (see 2 Cor. 4:3,4). God has given us powerful weapons of spiritual warfare that, when properly used, can remove those blinders. In many cases, however, ordinary prayers seem to have little effect because certain strongholds that have been erected have provided Satan a *legal right* to continue the evil work he is doing.

We are now realizing that the sins of past generations and the resultant iniquity present in our own generation have contributed to erecting and strengthening these strongholds much more than many of us could have imagined. Relating this to spiritual warfare, Scripture tells us, "The weapons of our warfare are not carnal but mighty in God for pulling down strongholds" (2 Cor. 10:4).

As I have mentioned previously, one category of these spiritual strongholds is "arguments," the translation of the Greek *logismous* (see v. 5), which implies that such strongholds come into being through certain human decisions and actions. Corporate sins such as Saul breaking the covenant with the Gibeonites or the American government breaking hundreds of equally valid covenants, or "treaties," with American Indians constitute strongholds that give the enemy a *legal right* to keep minds of the unsaved blinded to the gospel and also to steal, to kill and to destroy while he is doing this.

Identificational repentance helps to pull down such strongholds. Let me give you an example.

PACHANGAS HEAL SOBOBAS' PAST WOUNDS

The Pachangas and the Sobobas are two Indian nations located in what is now Southern California. Back before the arrival of the Europeans they had become bitter enemies. On one occasion, the Pachangas, who lived near the current San Diego, invaded the territory of the Sobobas, living in what is now Hemet, California, right across the San Jacinto Mountains from Palm Springs.

The warriors of both tribes locked into a fierce battle. As the struggle went on, the Soboba women and children escaped and hid themselves from danger deep in a canyon of the San Jacinto Mountains. The Pachanga warriors prevailed, and once they had defeated the Sobobas they followed the trail of the women and children into the canyon. They had no mercy. When they found them, they proceeded to slaughter every one of the defenseless Indians in cold blood. To this day the name of this place on the maps is listed as "Massacre Canyon."

This massacre furnished a stronghold for the devil. As the generations went by, the Sobobas as a group degenerated and became miserable. Destruction and death increased until not many years ago the Soboba Indian Reservation was classified by the United States Department of the Interior as the most violent of more than 300 reservations in the United States. They were averaging a murder a month, Indian killing Indian.

The Dwelling Place

Meanwhile, the whites settled in Hemet and it became a flourishing retirement community. Some years ago, Bob Beckett and his wife, Susan, moved into Hemet and founded The Dwelling Place Church. The Dwelling Place has enjoyed sustained growth and is now the spiritual home to more than 800 believers. Bob Beckett has emerged as one of the chief leaders of the Spiritual Warfare Network, and is much in demand as a conference speaker across the nation and in other parts of the world. He is a regular visiting lecturer in my Fuller Seminary classes, and I take my students on annual field trips to Hemet.

For many years, when his church was passing through some troubled waters, he held an annual spiritual warfare conference in Hemet featuring such experienced warriors as Cindy Jacobs and others. During those conferences, some whites repented of the abuses of their ancestors against the Indians, and significant reconciliation took place. Seeds of identificational repentance were planted. A handful of Sobobas and Pachangas were born again and they began to grow in their faith.

At one point, Bob Beckett discerned that his congregation was mature enough spiritually to tackle one of the region's most pressing social problems—the violence on the Soboba Reservation, located outside of town in the San Jacinto Mountains. Through the church's intercessors, they discerned God's timing and set a date for prophetic intercession, identificational repentance and certain prophetic acts on behalf of the Soboba Indians. Beckett called together his elders, his intercessors and the Christian Sobobas and Pachangas who were by now church members.

They met on a specific day, then drove their cars and vans to the mouth of Massacre Canyon and walked up the dry streamed to the place where the massacre had taken place and the innocent Soboba blood had been shed. As they stood in a group on that defiled land, they spent a good bit of time worshiping and exalting Jesus Christ as the rightful Lord of Massacre Canyon and of the Soboba Nation. They then went into an extended time of prayer, asking God to cleanse the land they were standing on of the blood guilt of past generations.

At the appropriate time, a Christian Pachanga publicly addressed a Christian Soboba, confessing the sins of the ancestors and asking forgiveness for the massacre. Not a dry eye could be seen in the canyon when the Soboba sincerely forgave the Pachanga, both of them identifying with their entire tribe and both acting on behalf of the leaders of a former generation.

In one accord, the group begged God to forgive the sin of the massacre, and then thanked Him for remitting the sin on the basis of the blood shed by Jesus Christ. To commemorate Jesus' death they all took Holy Communion, saving some of the wine, and symbolically pouring it out on the land. They claimed together that the power of the blood of Christ would overshadow the evil power of the innocent blood once shed there.

Staking the Ground

After communion, Bob Beckett performed a prophetic act by "staking the ground." He had brought along a 3-foot 2x2-inch oak stake, sharpened at one end, which had Scripture references inscribed on the four sides. In prayer and great faith, he drove the stake into the ground as a prophetic act to seal the spiritual transaction that had just taken place. When he finished, each person picked up a grapefruit-size stone from Massacre Canyon and drove in their cars and vans a short distance down the San Jacinto Mountains to the Soboba Reservation.

Beckett had previously secured permission from the Soboba chief to enter the reservation and pray for the Soboba people. Without this permission, they would not have dared to go close. One county social worker told me she never went into the reservation because whenever she tried, bullets were shot into her van. Violence was rampant and uncontrolled.

Once on the reservation, the group gathered at the burial ground. Previous spiritual mapping has indicated that the seat of the powers of darkness was located in the Soboba cemetery. There they had another sustained time of worship followed by powerful prayer. At the right moment, Bob Beckett drove a second stake into the ground, this time *breaking the curse of violence* over the Soboba Reservation as he was doing it. The group then solemnly piled up their grapefruit-size stones as a memorial, returned to their vehicles and went home.

What happened?

From Violence to Harvest

The public act of identificational repentance I have described took place in August 1992. Since then, and I am writing this four years later, not a single murder has been committed on the Soboba Reservation except for one that took place in a totally unrelated context. Acts of violence that were once the rule are now the exception. Social workers can come and go at will, and Satan's blinders have been removed. One-third of the Sobobas have now been converted, including a tribal shaman. He now serves as the head usher in The Dwelling Place Church!

On a recent field trip, my Fuller students and I saw a huge white tent in which evangelistic services were being held and people were being saved every night. Furthermore, reports are coming in that the revival is spreading to 10 other Indian Nations in Southern California.

Whether Southern Baptists or Japanese intercessors or Gibeonites or Promise Keepers or Soboba Indians, a rapidly growing number of people can testify that God truly has given us the power to heal the past!

Notes
1. George Otis Jr., *The Last of the Giants* (Grand Rapids: Chosen Books, 1991), p. 144.
2. Ibid., p. 225.
3. This is taken from an e-mail eyewitness report of the event by Gary Greig, who teaches Hebrew and Old Testament to seminary students at Regent University, Virginia Beach, Virginia.
4. Johannes Facius, *The Powerhouse of God* (Tonbridge, Kent, England: Sovereign World Ltd., 1995), p. 44.
5. Gary S. Greig, "Healing the Land: What Does the Bible Say About Identificational Repentance, Prayer, and Advancing God's Kingdom?" Unpublished paper written at Regent University (June 25, 1996), p. 9.
6. John Dawson, *Healing America's Wounds* (Ventura, Calif.: Regal Books, 1994), p. 30.
7. Ibid., p. 31.
8. *Charisma* (December 1993): 6.
9. Greig, "Healing the Land," p. 39.

▬ REFLECTION QUESTIONS ▬

1. In what sense is it correct to say that the Great Commission can be completed in our generation?
2. Why do you suppose that past generations of Christians did not recognize or teach identificational repentance?

3. Explain, as well as you can, the difference between sin and iniquity.
4. List some corporate sins you personally could identify with, even though they are not necessarily your own personal sins. Do you think it would be worthwhile to repent for any of these? Should others do it with you?

FURTHER RESOURCES

- *Healing America's Wounds* by John Dawson (Ventura, Calif.: Regal Books, 1994). This is the first ground-breaking textbook about identificational repentance. It is required reading!
- *The Powerhouse of God* by Johannes Facius (Tonbridge, England: Sovereign World, Ltd., 1995). See chapter 5, "Confessing the Sins of Nations."

Fresh Prayer Energy for Your Church

THE INCUBATOR FOR POWERFUL PRAYER ON ANY LEVEL IS the church. As the prayer energy in our churches increases, which it has been doing dramatically in the United States since about 1990, the effects will spread through the wider Christian community proportionately, and God's kingdom will advance irresistibly.

"LITTLE PRAYER, LITTLE POWER"

The movement toward powerful prayer began in China long before 1990. Partly as a result of that, China is in all probability the nation of the world that, at this writing, is seeing the greatest church growth week by week and month by month. Most of the churches there bear no outward resemblance at all to the churches in your community. Because the government of China is Marxist, it is not in the least favorable toward Christianity. It tries to convince the people that Christianity is a "foreign religion," but is having little success.

A relatively small number of Chinese Christians meet in church buildings something like ours, and are registered with the government. The majority gather in house churches, though, and attempt as much as possible to keep out of sight of the general public and of the government officials. Hundreds of new house churches begin meeting every week. Some researchers estimate that as many as 35,000 Chinese accept Jesus Christ as their Lord and Savior every single day!

How can this happen? How can some of the greatest church growth in the world be happening under a government bent on hindering the spread of the gospel in every way possible? It happens through prayer.

One researcher, who prefers to remain unnamed, reports: "It appears that the distinguishing feature of the present-day church growth in China is the disciplined prayer life of every believer. Chinese Christians pray to the Lord for (1) a watchful and praying spirit; (2) a burden to pray for others; (3) a time and place to pray; (4) energy to pray with fellow workers; and (5) the right words to use in prayer. In this manner they wish to be a trumpet to call all people to more prayer."[1] I love the way the Chinese use much of their prayer time to pray for more and better prayer time! No wonder their churches are on an upward spiral in both quantity and quality.

I recently received a report concerning an evangelist referred to as simply Brother Yeng. His assistant was preaching in an evangelistic meeting in a village where the gospel had never been preached. Some local gangsters who had heard of the meeting burst in to cause trouble. Brother Yeng took command of the pulpit as soon as he saw them coming in. He sensed the Holy Spirit telling him that the gangsters had decided to disrupt the meeting because they did not know the greatness of God. So what did he do? He prayed and said, "God, please show these people that you are a great and true God. Please perform a miracle!"

Sensing the flow of the Holy Spirit's power in answer to his prayer, Brother Yeng boldly said, "Is anyone here deaf?" A woman came forward bringing a deaf woman, who obviously had not heard the question. Brother Yeng prayed that God would heal the deaf woman, and she was immediately healed! He then invited all others who were deaf to come forward,

---

Chinese Christians have a widespread motto: *"Little prayer, little power; no prayer, no power."*

---

and, by God's grace, every one of them was healed right before the eyes of the audience.

Several people then rushed out of the meeting to bring back sick relatives. The gangsters? Amazed at what they were seeing, they rapidly changed their attitude toward the Christians and went home to bring back some of their sick family members as well. Before the end of the night, six of eight paralyzed people they prayed for were instantly healed!

The report goes on to say: "Because of the miracles, the whole village, including the gangsters, all believed in Jesus!"[2] Chinese Christians have a widespread motto: *"Little prayer, little power; no prayer, no power."*[3]

COULD YOUR CHURCH BECOME A HOUSE OF PRAYER?

Some of the most quoted words of Jesus were stated when He chased the money changers out of the Temple in Jerusalem.

He said, "It is written, 'My house shall be called a house of prayer'" (Matt. 21:13). Ever since then, many have applied it to their churches and have prayed, "God, please make our church a house of prayer."

As a result of the increasing momentum of the contemporary prayer movement, more and more churches in America and in other parts of the world now could conscientiously accept the designation "houses of prayer." I am sure the number of such churches is now larger than ever before in history, whether measured by sheer numbers or by percentage of existing churches.

One of the finest recent books about prayer in the local church is written by two friends of mine, Glen Martin and Dian Ginter. I love their title: *Power House: A Step-by-Step Guide to Building a Church That Prays* (Broadman & Holman). They talk about churches that are houses of prayer (as contrasted to churches that merely have a prayer ministry of some kind or other). They have formulated as good a description as I have found:

> The true powerful house of prayer will have prayer saturating every aspect of its individual and corporate life. Having significant prayer will be seen as the first thing to do when planning, when meeting, etc. There will be teaching on prayer from the pulpit, in Sunday School classes, and in small group settings. People will think of prayer as a major factor to be used at first to solve any problem. The whole congregation will be involved in prayer to some degree. Prayer will have a foundational positioning in the life of the individual and the church as a whole.[4]

Notice that Martin and Ginter stress that a church energized by prayer will see prayer in action both on the level of the individual church members and on the corporate level of the church as a whole. Surveys show that virtually all Christians (and also the majority of non-Christians) believe in prayer. Most of them do pray from time to time. Other than saying grace at meals and an occasional crisis prayer, though, too many Christians lack an ongoing attitude of prayer as a part of their normal lifestyles. Some do not take the time to set aside a daily time for talking to and listening to God. Members of churches that are houses of prayer tend to rise above such spiritual mediocrity and develop an ongoing communication with their Father. Life without prayer begins to feel strange.

THE KEY: THE SENIOR PASTOR

Only rarely, if ever, will a church wake up some morning and find that it has become a house of prayer. I have heard stories of this happening through a revival, but even in those cases the revival did not ordinarily penetrate through a prayer vacu-

---

A frequent saying of prayer leaders is, "What is *gained* by intercession must be *maintained* by intercession."

---

um. It almost always came as God's response to church members who were already praying. The transition to a house of prayer more than likely will happen through intentional actions of the leaders of the church. The key person for this is the senior pastor.

In helping pastors understand the dynamics of church growth for more than a quarter of a century, I have concluded that many of them are spending too much of their time and energy on the wrong things. I therefore attempt to help them readjust their priorities of leadership. I constantly encourage pastors to delegate more and more of the things they have been doing to gifted laypeople. I quote the Bible to them and remind them that a major role of pastors is to "[equip] the saints for the work of ministry" (Eph. 4:12). I also advise them that two things they *cannot* delegate, if their church is going to grow, are their leadership and their faith (or vision).

More recently, as a result of my studies of the prayer life of local churches, I have been forced, although reluctantly at first, to add a third item to the list of things a pastor should not delegate. If the church is ever to become a house of prayer, the senior pastor must cast the vision and assume the leadership of the church's prayer ministry. That does not mean the pastor cannot delegate the *administration* and the *implementation* of the prayer ministry. That *should* be delegated to intercessors and prayer leaders of various kinds.

All the church members should know without question that their pastor has prioritized prayer in his or her personal life and ministry. If this is the case, it will constantly surface in the pulpit. Hardly a sermon will be preached without acknowledging the power of prayer. In casual conversation, the pastor will turn the agenda to prayer as frequently as to any other topic. Testimonies to answered prayer will be a common part of church life. The pastor will brag to others, in the good sense of the word, about the prayer life of the people and the congregation as a whole and give the glory for it to God.

PRAYER LIFE IN THE PRAYER CAVE

In chapter 1 I told the story of how The Prayer Cave of Kiambu, Kenya, was planted through powerful prayer. A frequent saying of prayer leaders is, "What is *gained* by intercession must be *maintained* by intercession." Pastor Thomas Muthee must believe this, because there can be no question that prayer continues to be the number one priority of the church he pastors. His church is an extraordinary example of a house of prayer; and he, as the senior pastor, provides hands-on leadership for the ongoing prayer ministry.

Every Saturday morning the entire pastoral staff of The Prayer Cave, including the senior pastor, gathers with the intercessors

"Prayer is the means by which we become fused with God, to such an extent that God can easily flow into our affairs and we can easily flow into God's affairs."

and prays from 7:00 to 12:00. One of the elders has a full-time staff position just to administer and coordinate the prayer activities of the church. The designated intercession team of the church numbers about 400. Of them, 12 serve specifically as high level "crisis intercessors," which Thomas Muthee calls "the hit squad." They are highly gifted in discernment and prophetic intercession. They may spend three to four days at a time in the small prayer room called "the Powerhouse," which they constructed right next to the church. Intercessors occupy the Powerhouse, praying 24 hours every day. Once a month, a prayer retreat for intercessors only, called "Bush Ministry," meets in the forest for one day (which Africans call the "bush") from 8:30 A.M. to 5:00 P.M.

A prayer meeting called "Morning Glory" is held in the church from 5:00 A.M. to 6:30 A.M. every day. It is matched every evening with "Operation Prayer Storm." On Friday evenings the church sponsors an all-night prayer vigil from 9:00 P.M. to 6:00 A.M. The men's fellowship, the youth ministry, the women's group and the children's ministry each have a faithful prayer team to cover each particular area. Students in the church's Bible school are required to pray two hours a day as part of their schedule. In the Bible school, from 8:00 to 9:00 each morning a daily prayer meeting is scheduled, and from 2:00 to 3:00 each afternoon attendance at a "prayer school" is required of each student.

VERTICAL AND HORIZONTAL DIMENSIONS

I have heard Thomas Muthee say, "Why do we emphasize prayer so much in The Prayer Cave? Prayer is the means by which we become fused with God, to such an extent that God can easily flow into our affairs and we can easily flow into God's affairs."

Flowing into the affairs of God is an excellent analogy for a theology of prayer. This applies to the vertical dimension, our relationship with God. I also like what Glen Martin and Dian Ginter add to show how prayer can affect the horizontal, or interpersonal, dimension of church life. They say that prayer functions like oil. "Prayer provides the lubrication so that as a church, made up of different parts, all members can fit together perfectly, working together without friction, to perform a job which they could never accomplish on their own."[5]

It would be easy to assume that prayer is prayer without distinguishing between the many kinds of prayer that are necessary in a church. Muthee, for example, makes a clear distinction between those pray-ers who are designated as "intercessors," and those who are not. A smaller group among the intercessors are regarded as the "hit squad," who receive special, often confidential, prayer assignments.

Martin and Ginter point out that if prayer is like oil, different kinds of oil are needed for different kinds of machines. They say, "The same concept applies to prayer. There are different kinds of prayer for different kinds of situations. God has shown us how to pray for certain results, confess when appropriate, intercede for others, and do spiritual warfare in specific situations. Each fills a need and, when used appropriately, can be the very oil to make our lives and our churches run the best."[6]

PRAYER AND CHURCH GROWTH

I became interested in the prayer movement several years ago principally because I wanted to understand what relationship prayer had to the growth or nongrowth of churches. This would be expected because I am employed as a professor of church growth. I thought it would be an easy assignment and I would find that the churches that prayed the most would grow the most and churches that prayed less would grow less. After all, this is what I had been hearing in sermons about prayer. Most of my friends assumed it was true.

My first surprise was that hardly any solid research had previously been done about the subject. Apparently, the assumption of a direct positive correlation between prayer and church growth was so strong that research would seem redundant. I spent years and years studying growing American churches, interviewing their pastors and analyzing their growth dynamics.

In the first two books I wrote about American church growth, reference made to prayer is not substantial enough to find a place in the index! In the third, I wrote one paragraph about prayer in 218 pages! In church after church, almost all of them growing churches, prayer rarely surfaced as a significant subject in conversations with the pastors. My conclusion was that being a "house of prayer," as we have been defining it, apparently is not necessarily a prerequisite for church growth.

My doubts increased as I read three recent influential books by top leaders in evangelical Christianity. The first, by Tony Campolo and Gordon Aeschliman, is titled *101 Ways Your Church Can Change the World* (Regal Books). Not one of the

101 ways is prayer! The next two books were even more important to me because the authors are among the most prominent figures in the church growth movement. The authors, Bill Hybels and John Vaughan, are both personal friends of mine, and they know that the tone of these comments is not criticism, but rather a mutual admission that we may not always be as up front as we might in discussing the role of prayer in the growth of the church.

Bill Hybels is the pastor of what is widely regarded as the most influential church in America at this writing, Willow Creek Community Church in North Barrington, Illinois. A recent book, which he wrote with his wife, Lynne, is entitled *Rediscovering Church: The Story and Vision of Willow Creek Community Church* (Zondervan). It is a high quality and insightful book, carrying my personal endorsement on the back cover. Part One tells the story of the church. Part Two analyzes the growth principles employed, such as the 6 major elements comprising the vision of the church, a seven-step strategy for implementing the vision, 10 values that set the movement apart and 5 qualities of a true follower of Christ. Interestingly, of the 28 items, or growth dynamics, in Part Two, none is prayer!

John Vaughan directs the Megachurch Research Center in Bolivar, Missouri. He is recognized as possibly the leading figure in the country on megachurches, which by definition are churches consisting of more than 2,000 in attendance on weekends. I use his excellent book *Megachurches and America's Cities* (Baker) in my classes at Fuller Seminary. A key chapter in the book is "Predictable Changes in Growing Churches," in which Vaughan carefully analyzes characteristics of megachurches that seem to set them apart from smaller, nongrowing churches in the nation. He lists 20 of these growth principles, not one of which is prayer!

Both Hybels and Vaughan deeply believe in prayer and they practice prayer in their own lives. Bill Hybels has written a whole book about his prayer life: *Too Busy Not to Pray* (Inter-Varsity Press). If you asked either one of them what role prayer plays in the growth of churches, you would be likely to get a 20-minute monologue affirming with deep conviction that without powerful prayer large and influential churches could never have grown as they have. They would affirm that it is God, and God alone, who gives the increase. All this helped me begin to understand that just because pastors of growing churches may not include prayer on their lists of principal growth factors, it did not mean they necessarily considered prayer as incidental.

"PRAYER IS A *MAJOR* FACTOR"

It took my friend Thom Rainer of Southern Baptist Theological Seminary in Louisville, Kentucky, to give substance to what I had been expecting. He studied 576 of the most evangelistic churches he could find in America. He did not wait, though, to see if the pastors, left to themselves, would mention prayer as a factor. He included prayer on a list of factors he had the pastors evaluate. Much to my relief, he found that "Nearly 70 percent of the churches rated prayer as a *major* factor in their evangelistic success" (italics his).[7]

The following are some of the things the pastors of these growing churches said: "Prayer, corporate prayer, explains the evangelistic turnaround in our church"; "I believe the primary reason that God has His hand on our church is our commitment to the foundation of prayer"; "Our growth through conversions? It's the result of our prayer ministry that takes place seven days a week."[8]

Rainer says, "Therefore, we conclude, with conviction, that most evangelistically growing churches are also praying churches."[9]

Tommy Barnett of the huge First Assembly of God in

Phoenix, Arizona, tells how prayer and evangelism turned his church around. He preached about prayer and revival one Sunday and received a tremendously enthusiastic response from the congregation. Then he announced he was beginning a prayer meeting every Monday morning at 6:00. The next day no fewer than 1,000 people came just to pray.

Barnett says, "As we started praying, things began to happen in our church. Many people were saved. We put a pastor in the church 24 hours a day so people could bring the lost to get saved. Someone was also available around the clock to baptize the newly saved." Was this just a flash in the pan? No! Tommy Barnett adds, "The revival has never stopped. Our people began fasting, praying, and seeking God diligently, faithfully, and systematically. Then they go out and witness on the streets, winning people to Jesus Christ."[10]

The largest, fastest-growing church on the West Coast at this writing is Saddleback Valley Community Church in Orange County, California. Weekly attendance is currently running about 13,000. Prayer is a high priority for Pastor Rick Warren, a dear personal friend. In a recent letter to me Warren said, "We consider prayer and church growth to be so linked together that it is a membership requirement to commit to praying for the growth of Saddleback. If you won't commit to this you can't join because it is a part of the membership covenant that you must sign to become a member." Warren goes on to say, "I don't know of any other church in America that *requires* its members to pray for its growth!"[11]

At this point, I do not want to be misunderstood. I am not suggesting that the more prayer, the more church growth. Church growth is somewhat more complex than that. Many nongrowing churches have dynamic prayer ministries, but other factors are lacking. I agree with Rick Warren, who says, "Somebody needs to boldly state the obvious: Prayer alone will not grow a church." Warren affirms that "Prayer *is* essential," but he goes on to observe, "It takes far more than prayer to grow a church. It takes skilled action."[12] Having said that, let's move on to the basic rules of prayer.

PRAY ACCORDING TO THE RULES

As I have said many times, not all prayer is equal. This applies to the prayer life and ministry of a local church as much or more as to any other arena of prayer. In another book in *The Prayer Warrior Series, Churches That Pray* (see pages 46-56), I list four rules of prayer that bear repeating here, but have considerably less detail and include some other emphases. A pastor who wants to lead the church to become a true house of prayer should make sure these rules are woven into the very fabric of the congregation on every level.

Rule 1: Pray with Faith. "Without faith it is impossible to please [God]" (Heb. 11:6). Faith in prayer is believing that God will answer the prayer. Here is where the two-way prayer I discussed in chapter 2 becomes important. To the degree that we hear from God we can join Jesus, who said, "The Son can do nothing of Himself, but what He sees the Father do" (John 5:19). If we hear from God and know His will in a given situation, we then can pray with much more faith. "If we ask anything according to His will, He hears us" (1 John 5:14).

Nothing builds our faith in prayer more over the long haul than knowing our prayers are answered. One common fault I have found, including in churches that have strong prayer ministries, is that answers to prayers are not shared often enough with those who have prayed. It is one thing to believe that the Bible teaches God answers prayer. Most pray-ers do; but that is not enough. We have developed fairly efficient ways of putting current prayer *requests* into the hands of the people, but we are running far behind in doing the same with *answers* to prayers. Every positive answer we share builds the faith of those who prayed, and consequently their future prayers are more powerful because they have more faith.

One church I visited set aside a large room in which members of the congregation came to pray throughout the week. People were always praying there, some for longer times than others. On the right side of the room, a huge bulletin board was attached to the wall on which prayer requests were tacked. Intercessors removed the requests of their choice, prayed for them and fastened them back onto the bulletin board. The wall on the left side of the room contained another huge bulletin board on which the answered requests were tacked. Intercessors also helped themselves to the answers and lifted praises to God for His faithfulness and His power. Every answer built their faith and the prayer ministry flourished.

Rule 2: Pray with a Pure Heart. The effectiveness of prayer stands or falls on our relationship to God. The closer we are to God and the more intimate we are with the Father, the more accurately we can know His will and the more powerful our prayers will be. If we allow anything to come into our lives such as unconfessed sin, wrong attitudes, improper habits or questionable motives, we cannot sustain the relationship to God that we desire. If such is the case, we need to take immediate steps to clean up these things. God has given us ways and means to do this, although frequently we will need to seek the help of others who can minister to us and help us to be set free.

Fasting is one of the means God has provided for us to come into a closer relationship to Him. Alice Smith, one of Doris's and my personal intercessors, says, "Spiritual discernment is one of several benefits when fasting. Fasting sharpens our ability to discern the kingdom of light, and the kingdom of darkness. Discernment enhances our ability to see God's perspective in a given situation."[13]

Fasting was one of those things most Christian leaders I knew, including myself, glossed over until this remarkable decade of the 1990s came upon us. Now it seems we are bent on making up for lost time. The wide media coverage given to Bill Bright's first 40-day fast, and the subsequent prayer and fasting events that have drawn thousands of leaders have created a new climate. For the first time in my memory, fasting has become popular in America. When we do it, we now like to talk about it instead of keeping it a secret. Excellent books

---

The net result [of fasting], as I see it, is to draw God's people on a large scale closer to Him than we have been, and that will help purify our hearts so that our prayers can be more powerful.

---

about the subject, such as Elmer L. Towns's *Fasting for Spiritual Breakthrough* (Regal Books), are providing a deeper understanding of fasting than we have ever had. I will focus more on fasting in chapter 10.

The net result, as I see it, is to draw God's people on a large scale closer to Him than we have been, and that will help purify our hearts so that our prayers can be more powerful.

Rule 3: Pray with Power. After I was born again as an adult, I was nurtured in an evangelical tradition that acknowledged the Holy Spirit as part of the Trinity, but not much more. We became slightly embarrassed when groups such as Pentecostals seemed to talk too much about the Holy Spirit. We also tended to complain to each other that their emphasis on the Holy Spirit was taking glory away from Jesus, the person of the Trinity who rightly deserved it. What we failed to realize was that quenching the Spirit, which we were really doing (although we would have denied it), was, among other things, weakening our prayers. We understood only superficially what Paul meant when he said, "Praying always with all prayer and supplication *in the Spirit"* (Eph. 6:18, emphasis mine).

When Jesus first told His disciples He was going to leave them, it caused quite a commotion. Peter argued so strenuously that Jesus had to say, "Get behind Me, Satan!" (Matt. 16:23). When things calmed down, however, He told them it would be to their *advantage* if He left. How could that be?

Jesus said, "Nevertheless I tell you the truth. It is to your advantage that I go away; for if I do not go away, the Helper will not come to you" (John 16:7). To put it clearly, Jesus was telling His disciples that for the work He had called them to do, they would be better off with the immediate presence of the *Third* Person of the Trinity than they would with the *Second* Person.

I am not alone these days in recognizing the crucial role of the Holy Spirit in our lives and ministries. As a result, I have shed many of my previous inhibitions in talking about the power and the gifts of the Holy Spirit and overtly appropriating them in my life and ministry. My new enthusiasm for spiritual things is not without its price. Many of my old friends, although not exactly rejecting me, have decided they would be more comfortable to keep me at arm's length because I seem to them to be "too charismatic." Even so, I still believe that to the degree we receive the fullness of the Holy Spirit and operate in all the gifts of the Spirit, the more powerful our prayers become.

Rule 4: Pray with Persistence. Let me elaborate on this rule by presenting a personal testimony from Singapore. Gordon Tan is a Singapore medical doctor who had decided he could acquire everything he ever needed in life without God, until his beautiful wife, Kim Li, developed a form of cancer. Tests showed that a certain hormone had reached a dangerous level of 10,000 units/liter. If it did not come down in a few weeks, radical treatment would be necessary. For the first time, Gordon Tan decided to pray to Jesus, which he did. The next week the level remained at 10,000 units. He said, "I continued praying but felt as though I was praying to a wall. There was no response from God. I felt abandoned by Jesus, forgetting that it was I who had earlier abandoned Him."

In a few weeks, the count went up to 20,000 units, precipitating a crisis. Of five doctors handling the case, four called for immediate cancer treatment. One was willing to allow one more week, and Gordon chose that option. He says, "At this stage, I was in pieces. My whole life appeared shattered. Where was this God I had prayed to for four whole weeks?" In desperation, he called the Anglican bishop and asked him to come to the hospital, anoint his wife with oil and pray for her healing. When he did, Kim Li felt a power surging through her body that would have caused her to collapse if she had not been sitting.

Dr. Tan says, "That night, a broken man, I came before God as a child. For four whole weeks I had been calling my own terms: 'Heal her! Heal her!' For four whole weeks I had bargained, 'Lord heal her. Heal her and I will do whatever you want.' That night I surrendered all to him. Tomorrow would be the results of the crucial blood test. I prayed, 'Lord Jesus, I have fallen from a cliff. I am two inches from the rocks. If you do not save me now, I am finished. But, Lord, thy will be done.'"

The next day the blood test went down to 1,400 and soon it was down to zero. Kim Li had been miraculously healed!

Reflecting on what at first seemed to be unanswered prayer, Gordon Tan rejoiced that he had the persistence, although having a low level of faith, to continue beseeching God. He summarizes it by saying, "During that time my pride was slowly broken until my spirit was like putty before him. But just before

I was about to snap, God saved me. The Lord needed that time to break me till I came to him as a child so that he could build me up again."[14] Dr. Tan had learned the fourth rule of prayer: persistence.

MAKING IT HAPPEN

I won't extend this chapter by attempting to catalog the increasing numbers of practical, effective and exciting ideas that are emerging to help transform your local church into a house of prayer. In the resource section at the end of the chapter, you will find valuable tools to help make it happen.

I think I should highlight one concept, however, that seems to me to have the potential of being the most powerful thing local churches could do to multiply the effectiveness of their prayers for their churches, for their communities and for the unreached peoples of the world in this decade. I refer to "local church prayer rooms."

Although no overall coordination of the movement is in place as yet, some estimate that up to 2,000 local churches in the United States have already installed prayer rooms or prayer chapels or upper rooms or prayer centers or whatever they might be called. It seems the two denominations that have the largest number of prayer rooms are Southern Baptists and United Methodists.

The most prominent national leader of this movement I know of is Terry Teykl, former pastor of Aldersgate United Methodist Church in College Station, Texas, and founder of Renewal Ministries. Terry is actively promoting the prayer room movement across the nation, and he has written a textbook about the subject, *Making Room to Pray*. In it he says, "A place or center designed for this makes continual prayer a possibility for any congregation. In this way the church and city can be 'soaked' in prevailing prayer."[15]

Your church probably has the potential to find a room that can be designated as a prayer room. Kenwood Baptist Church of Cincinnati, Ohio, has a prayer room that operates 24 hours a day, seven days a week. Here is their description of a prayer room: "Furnished as a warm, inviting room, there is a small altar area, comfortable chairs, floor pillows, a meeting table, and five study tables set up as prayer stations. The prayer stations have up-to-date information to stimulate prayer about various needs such as missions, staff, congregation needs, government leaders, etc."[16] The following diagram is a floor plan of the church's prayer room:

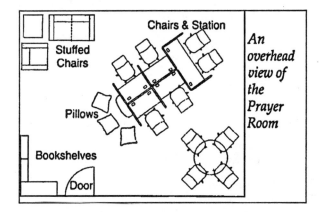

A typical prayer room has one or two telephone lines. Some will be able to afford a dedicated fax line, and some a computer equipped for e-mail and access to the World Wide Web. It is a place, as Terry Teykl says, "where prayer can happen—a room, a site, a meeting hall—just as the disciples met in the Upper Room. In this actual room people can pray, cry, petition, wait, be quiet, intercede, and believe to receive from God."[17]

A local church prayer room that aims for 24-hour-a-day staffing is one of the highest commitments to prayer a church can make. It also has extremely high potential for returns that benefit the kingdom of God. It constitutes a major step toward transforming an ordinary church into a house of prayer.

Could your church become a "house of prayer"?

■ REFLECTION QUESTIONS ■

1. On a scale of 1 to 10, where would you rank your church as a "house of prayer"? Why?
2. Can you name some pastors who seem to give a higher profile to prayer than others do? What do they do differently?
3. If God does not answer your prayer the first time, do you pray again? How long do you keep praying?
4. What are some things that could be done in your church to raise the level of powerful prayer?

Notes

1. This report is found in Carl Lawrence with David Wang, *The Coming Influence of China* (Gresham, Oreg.: Vision House Publishing, Inc., 1996), p. 52.
2. From the Internet "New Wine China Ministries," <new-wine@grmi.org> (February 25, 1996).
3. Lawrence, *The Coming Influence,* p. 52.
4. Glen Martin and Dian Ginter, *Power House: A Step-by-Step Guide to Building a Church That Prays* (Nashville: Broadman & Holman Publishers, 1994), p. 17.
5. Ibid., p. 15.
6. Ibid., p. 16.
7. Thom Rainer, *Effective Evangelistic Churches* (Nashville: Broadman & Holman Publishers, 1996), p. 67.
8. Ibid., p. 69.
9. Ibid., p. 71.
10. Tommy Barnett, "Revival Begins with Prayer," *Enrichment* (Fall 1996): 24.
11. Personal letter to the author from Rick Warren, dated December 20, 1996.
12. Rick Warren, *The Purpose Driven Church* (Grand Rapids: Zondervan Publishing House, 1995), p. 58.
13. Alice Smith, *Power Praying: Instruction on Prayer & Fasting* (Alice Smith, 7710-T Cherry Park Drive, Suite 224, Houston, TX 77095, 1996), p. 2.
14. Gordon Tan, "The Healing of Kim Li Tan," *Asian Report* (September-October 1985): 11-12.
15. Terry Teykl, *Making Room to Pray: How to Start and Maintain a Prayer Room in Your Church* (Anderson, Ind.: Bristol Books, 1993), p. 9.

16. Karen Navera, ed., *An Invitation to the Prayer Room at Kenwood Baptist Church*, pamphlet published in 1995.
17. Teykl, *Making Room to Pray*, p. 16.

FURTHER RESOURCES

- *Churches That Pray* by C. Peter Wagner (Ventura, Calif.: Regal Books, 1993). This is the other book in *The Prayer Warrior Series* that will provide many more principles and ideas about how to turn your church into a "house of prayer."
- *Making Room to Pray* by Terry Teykl (Anderson, Ind.: Bristol Books, 1993). This is a thorough, how-to manual for starting and maintaining a prayer room in your church.
- *The Praying Church Sourcebook* by Alvin Vander Griend (1990) (Church Development Resources, 2850 Kalamazoo Avenue, SE, Grand Rapids, MI 49560). This three-ring notebook contains virtually every idea ever thought of for prayer activities in your church. I highly recommend it. Order from the above address.
- *Power House* by Glen Martin and Dian Ginter (Nashville: Broadman & Holman Publishers, 1994). The subtitle says it all: *A Step-by-Step Guide to Building a Church That Prays.* I know of no better book about this subject.
- *The Praying Church* by Sue Curran (Shippensburg, Pa.: Treasure House, 1987). This is the best book I have found about developing the corporate prayer life of your church. It contains vital ideas for your church prayer meeting.

God's Gift of Personal Intercessors for Leaders

MY FRIEND JOHN DEVRIES OF MISSION 21 INDIA recently brought back a field report I have not forgotten. One of the four executive pastors of the huge New Life Church of Bombay is Willie Sloan. Sloan and his wife had worked as church-planting missionaries in Nagpur, India, for 10 years. Their story was much like that of many other missionaries—they seemed to face serious opposition of almost every kind. They tried every human method they knew, but by 1992, after 10 strenuous years, they could point to only six small house churches as the fruit of their labor. I know some missionaries who would try to convince their supporters that such results were all that could be expected considering the circumstances, but Willie Sloan was not among them. Frankly, he was upset.

FULL-TIME INTERCESSORS

So in 1992 the Sloans tried something that was new for them. They began to employ full-time intercessors who would constantly keep them before God's throne. By October 1995, 20 women and 2 men were praying full time each day. The intercessors were those who understood the principles of strategic-level spiritual warfare and whose prayers were known to be of the more powerful kind. During the three years they were receiving personal intercession, the Sloans, using the same methods as before, were successful in planting no fewer than 180 house churches! Instead of planting 6 new churches in 10 years, they were now planting 6 new churches a month!

I know of no pastors or other Christian leaders who would not desire to see that kind of incremental effectiveness in their ministries. Although certainly other variables are likely to enter the picture, I know of no step a pastor or missionary or seminary professor or other leader could take that has a higher potential for increasing ministry power than recruiting a team of personal intercessors. They, of course, do not have to be full-time employees as were those in India, but the right ones will still be highly committed.

I regard my book *Prayer Shield,* which is a textbook about this subject, as the most important book I will probably ever write for pastors. When it was first published, my friend Elmer Towns read it and wrote a letter to me, saying, "Peter, when you die this will be the book, among the three or four dozen you have written, for which you will be the most remembered." I would agree with Elmer.

Speaking of seminary professors, I mentioned my friend Thom Rainer's research about prayer and church growth in the last chapter. During the past few years, Thom has emerged as one of the .300 hitters, so to speak, of the church growth movement. Before becoming the dean of the Billy Graham School of Evangelism, Church Growth and Missions at Southern Baptist Theological Seminary, he pastored a large, rapidly growing church. The following is Thom Rainer's testimony:

> In 1992, primarily because of Peter Wagner's influence, I began to pray that God would raise up intercessors for my ministry and my family. I was the pastor of a large church in Birmingham, Alabama. As I reflect upon those days, I now see that they were the most difficult times I had known in pastoral ministry. But God did call several people to intercede daily for me. I began to know the power of prayer for my ministry as I had never known before. God was once again showing me the priority and power of prayer.[1]

THE MOST UNDERUTILIZED SOURCE OF SPIRITUAL POWER

I clearly recall the days, back in 1987, when I first received the assignment from the Lord to research, teach and write about prayer. Prayer was a totally unfamiliar field for me, so I began to build a library and to read as many of the books about prayer as I could to make up for lost time. I now have almost 10 shelves of books about prayer. One of my early objectives, among other things, was to try to identify the areas within the field of prayer that had not attracted much attention at that time. One of them, which I soon discerned, was this matter of intercession for Christian leaders.

As far as I can remember, the only reference I found to intercession for leaders was a chapter in a book by E. M. Bounds, the most prolific writer about prayer in American history. In his book *Power Through Prayer,* written in 1912, he includes a chapter called "Preachers Need the Prayers of the

People." It may have been short (only 2 pages out of a total of 568 pages in his complete works), but, as is characteristic of Bounds, it was straightforward.

Bounds says, "Somehow the practice of praying in particular for the preacher has fallen into disuse or become discontinued. Occasionally have we heard the practice arraigned as a disparagement of the ministry, being a public declaration by those who do it of the inefficiency of the ministry." What does Bounds think of this? "It offends the pride of learning and self-sufficiency, perhaps, and these ought to be offended and rebuked in a ministry that is so derelict as to allow them to exist."[2]

If praying for the pastor was in disuse in 1912, the same could also be said of 1987. It might well be that it had not come into prominent use in many churches during the 75-year interval. I have yet to see evidence that it was practiced in any intentional or overt way in the Body of Christ throughout the centuries of Church history. I became bold enough to state on the first page of my book *Prayer Shield* that *the most underutilized source of spiritual power in our churches today is intercession for Christian leaders.*

DISCOVERING THE NEED FOR A PRAYER SHIELD

I might never have noticed the absence of writings about personal intercession for leaders had it not been for a series of circumstances in my life God used to make me aware of the value of personal intercession. In 1982, I founded an adult Sunday School class at Lake Avenue Congregational Church of Pasadena, California, which I subsequently taught for 13 years. Named "The 120 Fellowship," my wife, Doris, and I soon became aware that this was probably the first Christian group we had been associated with during three decades of ministry that seemed to be spontaneously providing a substantial prayer covering for us. That was quite a few notches above the expected prayers of Christian people for their leaders.

A life-changing event took place in 1983 when I experienced a free fall from a ladder in my garage. I fell about 12 feet to the cement floor on the back of my head and neck. It could well have taken my life, and it might have, had it not been for the prayers of a young woman from the Sunday School class, Cathy Schaller. She had heard from the Lord, 10 miles away, that someone important to her was in a life-or-death situation and she needed to intercede immediately. This was new to her also, but she obeyed God and for 20 minutes she prayed fervently for legions of angels to protect whoever it was from death at exactly the time I was falling to the floor. That initiated a period of seven years during which Cathy served as the principal personal intercessor for Doris and me. The ripple effect also spread through the class, however, and many others started praying for us in a special way.

By the time I began researching prayer in 1987, I had become close personal friends with John Maxwell, pastor of Skyline Wesleyan Church in San Diego, California. Among other things, he told me he had recruited no fewer than 100 men in his church who were committed to pray for him and his ministry on a highly accountable and sustained basis. I made a special point of studying what was happening at Skyline, and no one has influenced me more than John Maxwell in developing personal prayer partners of my own.

At this writing, Doris and I have more than 200 active prayer partners. One of them we call our "I-1" intercessor, and 21 are "I-2" intercessors. The rest we regard as "I-3" intercessors. We consider all of them highly important, but we relate more closely to the I-1s and I-2s. I have a picture of each of them pasted on the inside cover of my Bible, and I mention them in my prayers each day, thanking God for the divine power that comes through their ministry on our behalf.

VICTORY THROUGH THE INTERCESSOR

Just about everyone who has spent some time in Sunday School has heard the story, from Exodus 17, of how Joshua defeated Amalek in the Valley of Rephidim while Moses was on a nearby mountain interceding for him. Joshua has gone down in military history as the general who won the battle. We know,

---

Two things need to happen simultaneously for victory in the ministry: The pastor or leader must pray more, and the pastor or leader must learn to receive intercession.

---

though, that the feat was accomplished, not through superior military skill or bravery, but by the power of God. The chief human instrument for the flow of divine power into the Valley of Rephidim was Moses, the intercessor. When Moses' hands were up, Joshua was winning; when they were down, Joshua was losing. Aaron and Hur came alongside and did what was necessary to support the intercessor and the battle was won.

The Battle of Rephidim was won by prayer. How much do you think Joshua was praying that day? Obviously, it was very little, if at all. Joshua reminds me of many pastors today. They are the ones on the front lines. They are fighting the daily battles on the front lines of the kingdom of God. It is not easy. No other profession records a higher percentage of burnout cases. Research shows that the pastor is the number one factor, among many, for the growth or nongrowth or for the health or weakness of the local church. No wonder the devil seeks out pastors.

Terry Teykl says, "We are at war with an unseen spiritual

enemy who opposes pastors at every turn."[3] Their battle will not be won, though, by their knowledge of Greek or their mastery of systematic theology, or their pulpit communication skills or any other good human quality. They need help from God just as Joshua did.

E. M. Bounds says, "Air is not more necessary to the lungs than prayer is to the preacher. It is absolutely necessary for the preacher to pray. It is an absolute necessity that the preacher be prayed for."[4] Notice that two things need to happen simultaneously for victory in the ministry: The pastor or leader must pray more, and the pastor or leader must learn to receive intercession.

PASTORS SHOULD PRAY MORE

Awhile ago I conducted a research project about American pastors and found that the average pastor prays 22 minutes a day. This did not surprise me too much, but I was a bit startled to find that more than one out of four pastors pray less than 10 minutes a day! When I present seminars or classes for pastors, they all nod their heads and identify with those numbers. Furthermore, they all know they need more prayer.

Before I go on to talk about receiving the prayers of intercessors in my classes, I admonish the pastors I am teaching to exercise more self-discipline and to make a firm decision to pray more. It boils down to their choice. Everyone has 24 hours a day, and it is ultimately up to each one of us how we decide to manage that time. At the end of the day, we have been doing what we have considered, for whatever reasons, the highest priority items. The excuse "I was too busy to pray today" is about as weak as they get. It would have been more honest to say, "I had higher priority things on my agenda today than to pray."

Bill Hybels of Willow Creek Community Church, whom I mentioned in the last chapter, agrees. That is why he wrote a whole book about prayer, titled *Too Busy Not to Pray*. He is a good example, because few pastors could have been busier than Hybels was while leading his church to become the largest one in the United States. For a long time, Bill Hybels thought he could assume prayer would simply be a part of his lifestyle as he went about a daily routine. It did not work, though. Hybels says, "I used to try to pray and receive God's leadings on the run. It became obvious to me that my pace of life outstripped my capacity to analyze it....At the end of a day I would wonder if my work had any meaning at all."[5]

His solution? "I developed my own disciplined approach to stillness before God. It is the only spiritual discipline I have ever really stuck with, and I am not tempted to abandon it because it has made my life so much richer."[6] Every morning Bill Hybels spends 30 to 60 minutes of clock time in a secluded place, just with the Lord. He has discovered that "People who are really interested in hearing from God must pay a price: they must discipline themselves to be still before God."[7]

But That Is Not Enough

Pastors or Christian leaders do not possess the spiritual self-sufficiency necessary to carry them in their ministries or in their personal lives. Without mentioning any names, the pastor who was involved in one of the highest visibility moral downfalls in recent years professed to pray for two and one-half hours daily. In retrospect, however, he admitted that one of his weaknesses was his reluctance to receive meaningful personal spiritual support from other members of the Body of Christ.

E. M. Bounds says, "The more the preacher's eyes are opened to the nature, responsibility, and difficulties in his work, the more he will see, and if he be a true preacher the more he will feel the necessity of prayer; not only the increasing demand to pray himself, *but to call on others to help him by their prayers*" (italics mine).[8]

Pastors have failed to seek personal intercession for many reasons, but I believe the number one reason is ignorance. I can cite repeated cases of pastors who first heard about personal intercessors in one of my seminars. They formed prayer teams in a week or two, and later wrote about the tremendous difference it made. They said, "Why didn't I ever know about this before?"

Cindy Jacobs of Generals of Intercession, who is one of Doris's and my closest prayer partners, writes, "Whenever those in ministry call me with tremendous burdens on their shoulders, one of the first questions I ask is, 'Do you have personal prayer partners?' They will invariably say, 'I have people who tell me they pray for me on a regular basis.' And I say, 'But do they know your needs on an intimate level?' Only a handful have even thought of mobilizing personal intercession."[9]

Terry Teykl, one of America's foremost prayer leaders, was one of those pastors suffering burnout while he was pastoring the rapidly growing Aldersgate United Methodist Church in College Station, Texas. "In 1987," Teykl says, "I went through a personal crisis and burnout....There simply weren't enough hours in the day. At the time, I was a devout codependent who was committed to a ministerial model of rugged individualism." The situation was serious enough to demand counseling. After some time off, Terry came to realize that, as he puts it, "Because I was laboring under an image of total self-sufficiency, I had been remiss in asking members of my own church to pray for me!"[10]

When Terry Teykl confessed his weaknesses from the pulpit and asked his people to pray for him, things began to change. He says, "My life took a dramatic turn for the better. People began praying and I entered into an entirely new relationship with the flock. I would not have remained in ministry without the prayers of these saints."[11]

WHO ARE THE INTERCESSORS?

Those who are familiar with my book *Your Spiritual Gifts Can Help Your Church Grow* (Regal Books) will know that I think it is important to distinguish between spiritual gifts and Christian roles. To illustrate: All Christians must live a life characterized by faith, although only a limited number have the *gift* of faith (see 1 Cor. 12:9). Every believer should tithe his or her income and give generous offerings over and above that, but some have a *gift* of giving (see Rom. 12:8) that goes beyond what is expected of the others. Everyone who is born again should be a witness of the saving power of Christ, but a few have a *gift* of evangelist (see Eph. 4:11). By the same token, every Christian has a role to pray and to intercede, but God has given to some the *gift* of intercession.

Intercessors pray longer than the average Christian, they pray with more intensity, they enjoy prayer more, they see more frequent answers to their prayers and they have spiritual ears to hear from God more readily than most. I think virtually every church has been provided with some individuals who have the gift of intercession. The best I can estimate, they may represent about 5 percent of the membership of the average church. In many churches, though, the intercessors have never been recognized. Some pastors have no idea any such thing as specially gifted and called intercessors exists. Others may know about intercessors, but they feel threatened by them because intercessors are known to hear from God regularly and they may hear some things about the church the pastor has not yet heard.

If I were Satan, I would give high priority to keeping pastors and intercessors apart. If ignorance would do it, that would be fine. For those who are not ignorant, though, I would try to produce conflict and estrangement. It is a fact that many intercessors, because they are acutely aware of specific details of the invisible world, develop patterns of behavior and conversation a bit out of the ordinary. Admittedly, some have a tendency toward what could be considered as flakiness, although I have not yet met an intercessor unwilling to receive correction.

Alice Smith, our I-1 intercessor, says, "Because of the spiritual burdens they sometimes bear, intercessors can easily

> **The person who has the highest spiritual authority in the church is the pastor. Those who hear most from God, frequently more than the pastor, are the intercessors. Put them together, and you have a winning combination.**

become moody. Heaviness or depression can creep into the intercessor's life, so it is necessary to ask the Holy Spirit whether a burden is genuine or an attack of the enemy."[12]

Some intercessors are shy; they have perceived that they are rejected; they know they are different and think they are alone, and therefore they pull into their shells. They continue to pray, but their prayers carry only a fraction of the effectiveness they could have if they flowed out of a quality relationship with the pastor for whom they are praying.

CONNECTING PASTORS WITH INTERCESSORS

Connecting pastors with intercessors is like connecting a quarterback with a wide receiver. They are different from each other in skills and roles as well as physical characteristics. Each one alone could do relatively little for the team. Together, though, they score a touchdown. The person who has the highest spiritual authority in the church is the pastor. Those who hear most from God, frequently more than the pastor, are the intercessors. Put them together, and you have a winning combination.

For years I have observed the incredible relationship between John Maxwell and his I-1 intercessor, Bill Klassen. When John became the pastor of Skyline Wesleyan Church in San Diego, this stranger managed to get an appointment with him. He told John he was an intercessor who prayed for pastors, and God had sent him there to pray for John. As anyone who knows Maxwell will tell you, this is not the usual way John initiates relationships. This, however, was not a usual meeting. The Holy Spirit was there with power and He bonded them in a supernatural way.

Maxwell says, "Neither of our lives has ever been the same since that meeting. Bill became my personal prayer and accountability partner after that, and he went on to help me organize a prayer partner ministry at Skyline, a group of people who prayed for me every day during my fourteen years there and who met in small groups in a tiny room at church every Sunday to cover the services with prayer."[13]

I relate this incident to illustrate how intercessors hear from God and speak blessing into the lives of those for whom they pray. Fourteen years went by, and God was moving John out of the local church into a national training ministry. He tells of how he made that difficult decision, and Bill Klassen was one of the first who knew about it.

When John told Bill he had made his decision to leave the church, big tears came into Bill's eyes and he said, "John, you're exactly right. In fact I had a passage I wanted to share with you when you told me because I knew it was coming." He opened his Bible to Isaiah 43:18,19, which was already marked, and read, "Do not remember the former things, nor consider the things of old. Behold, I will do a new thing; now it shall spring forth; shall you not know it?" They embraced and wept together, having the assurance from God that the way they were heading was the right way.[14]

In the last few paragraphs I have highlighted those who have the gift of intercession. We should not draw the conclusion, however, that people who do not have the gift cannot enroll as personal intercessors for leaders as well. When Doris and I first formed our closer circles of prayer partners, which we call I-1 and I-2, probably not more than half had the gift of intercession, and the others simply used their Christian roles as pray-ers and supported us tremendously. Many on our broader I-3 list do not have the gift of intercession. As the years have passed, it turns out that presently of 22 I-1 and I-2 intercessors, only 3 do not have the gift. I will admit, though, that our team is quite a bit above the average, and we thank God daily for them.

PETER AND PAUL HAD PERSONAL INTERCESSORS

One morning King Herod woke up and decided he would put two Christian leaders on his hit list: James and Peter. He succeeded in killing James, but not Peter. He kept Peter in jail, and was preparing to execute him when an angel entered the jail cell and escorted Peter past the maximum security guards and into freedom without anyone knowing what was happening. How could something like this occur?

The Bible says something about Peter it does not say about James: "Constant prayer was offered to God for [Peter] by the church" (Acts 12:5). The prayer meeting was held in the home of Mary, the mother of Mark. I have a hypothesis with which some may agree and some may disagree. Mary could well have been Peter's personal intercessor. Whether James had a personal intercessor we cannot know. When Peter was in prison, the same thing happened then as would happen today if I went to jail. The intercessors would be on red alert and they would call in all the reinforcements available to do battle on my behalf in the invisible world. I have no doubt that what happened in Mary's house literally saved Peter's life.

When Paul writes to the believers in Rome, he pleads for personal intercession: "Now I beg you, brethren, through the Lord Jesus Christ, and through the love of the Spirit, that you strive together with me in your prayers to God for me" (Rom. 15:30).

Paul asks the believers in Ephesus to be "praying always with all prayer and supplication in the Spirit,...for me, that utterance may be given to me" (Eph. 6:18,19).

Paul commends the believers in Philippi for their prayers on his behalf (see Phil. 1:19) and mentions by name Euodia and Syntyche (see 4:2), who, I believe, were Paul's personal intercessors. This probable relationship has been hidden from many Bible students by two things. For one, the two women seemed at the moment to be at odds with each other for some reason and this has attracted a good bit of the attention of preachers and commentators. Second, our usual English translations have Paul describing these women as those "who labored with me in the gospel" (Phil. 4:3), and hide the literal meaning of the Greek, which really is "who did spiritual warfare on my behalf."[15] This sounds a lot like the ordinary job description of personal intercessors.

OBTAINING INTERCESSORS

Virtually nothing about the subject of personal intercession for pastors and leaders was available in 1987, but we have many fine resources now. These are listed in the resource section at the end of the chapter. Several of these books include lists of steps, and every list is good. I am not sure, however, that every list fits every situation, and that is why I have hesitated in making a list of my own. What might work for a local church pastor might not work for a seminary professor like me, and what might work for me might not work for the leader of an evangelistic association.

We who are leaders must (1) *obtain* personal intercessors, and (2) *maintain* personal intercessors.

I am sure, however, that two principles will apply across the board. We who are leaders must (1) *obtain* personal intercessors, and (2) *maintain* personal intercessors. I have worded this intentionally to imply that if something is going to happen, it will ordinarily happen at the initiative of the leader. Certainly there are exceptions to this rule, such as the manner in which Bill Klassen approached John Maxwell. If it does happen that way, though, it is absolutely essential that the pastor be open to receiving intercession before a Bill Klassen introduces himself. Unfortunately, not all pastors are open to having intercessors.

A major reason some pastors shy away from personal intercession is that they fear the personal vulnerability that will likely occur if they open themselves to the serious intercession of another person. This is a legitimate concern because such is not only likely to happen, indeed, it *should* happen. That is why the choice of intercessors and cementing the relationship is such a serious matter. Doris and I believe that divine initiative is called for in selecting an I-1 intercessor. God takes the action, and we simply recognize that His hand is moving. We accept new I-2 intercessors only after months of waiting on God. The pathway for I-3 intercessors is more open, but we still look for certain indications before relating to new ones.

Obstacles are rapidly being overcome, and I regularly receive reports of pastors who are connecting with intercessors. Alice Smith is noticing the same thing. She says, "Christian leaders are learning about the nature and calling of intercession. It is exciting to see pastoral leadership become more aware of the ministry of intercession. Their interest in developing intercessors and appropriating their gifts in the Church will encourage the rest of the Body to pray."[16]

MAINTAINING INTERCESSORS

John Maxwell says, "If you are going to develop lasting relationships with your prayer partners, transparency is fundamental. When you are transparent, you communicate that you trust and value them and their prayers. By confessing your sins, needs, and weaknesses, you show them how they can pray for you. And you open the door for them to be transparent too."[17]

When Doris and I make a covenant with people to serve as I-1 or I-2 intercessors, we communicate to them both in person and in writing that from that time on, we are giving God permission to tell the intercessors anything and everything about our personal lives. Because most intercessors are prophetic, this means *they know!* We trust them fully, though, because we have made sure they have the spiritual maturity to handle whatever God tells them; and because they love us, they use it for our blessing.

It is not unusual for an intercessor to call and say, "I prayed for you almost three hours yesterday afternoon, and it was a powerful time. Here are a couple of things I believe God wants you to know. There are some other things, however, that God instructed me to keep to myself for now." It is true that some of our intercessors know more about us than we know ourselves; and I would not have it any other way.

Communication with the intercessors is essential. Our I-1 and I-2 intercessors have our unlisted home phone number and are encouraged to call at any time of day and night. We write a personal letter to all intercessors about every four or five weeks, aided by Jane Rumph of Pasadena, California, who serves as an I-2 intercessor and the coordinator of our prayer partners ministry. I frequently send separate mailings to I-1 and I-2 intercessors when a crisis or important decision is imminent. I have no hesitation to send them copies of confidential correspondence, for that is the correspondence ordinarily needing the most prayer. Apart from our personal family, these are the most important people in our lives.

God has given us leaders a precious gift of personal intercessors. It is my prayer that more and more pastors and other Christian leaders around the world will receive that gift in gratitude, and that as a result God's kingdom will advance as never before.

■ REFLECTION QUESTIONS ■

1. Were you surprised to read that the average American pastor prays 22 minutes a day? Do you know many pastors who pray more?
2. Who are some people you could name who seem to have the spiritual gift of intercession?
3. To your knowledge, does your pastor have some special people relating to him or her as personal prayer partners?
4. Discuss in your own words why the devil would want to keep pastors and intercessors apart.

Notes
1. Thom Rainer, *Effective Evangelistic Churches* (Nashville: Broadman & Holman Publishers, 1996), p. 66.

2. E. M. Bounds, *The Complete Works of E. M. Bounds on Prayer* (Grand Rapids: Baker Book House, 1990), p. 486.
3. Terry Teykl, *Preyed on or Prayed For: Hedging Your Pastor in Prayer* (Anderson, Ind.: Bristol Books, 1994), p. 139.
4. Bounds, *The Complete Works*, p. 486.
5. Bill Hybels, *Too Busy Not to Pray* (Downers Grove, Ill.: InterVarsity Press, 1988), p. 119.
6. Ibid.
7. Ibid., pp. 117-118.
8. Bounds, *The Complete Works*, p. 486.
9. Cindy Jacobs, *Possessing the Gates of the Enemy* (Grand Rapids: Baker Books, 1991; revised edition, 1994), p. 157.
10. Teykl, *Preyed On or Prayed For*, p. 17.
11. Ibid., p. 18.
12. Alice Smith, *Beyond the Veil: God's Call to Intimate Intercession* (Houston: SpiriTruth Publishing, 1996), p. 59.
13. John Maxwell, *Partners in Prayer* (Nashville: Thomas Nelson Publishers, 1996), p. 3.
14. This story was narrated by John Maxwell in the Injoy Life Club tape, vol. 12, no. 2, 1996.
15. For more detail about this exegesis, see my commentary on Acts, *Blazing the Way* (Vol. 3) (Ventura, Calif.: Regal Books, 1995), pp. 97-98.
16. Smith, *Beyond the Veil*, pp. 59-60.
17. Maxwell, *Partners in Prayer*, pp. 135-136.

FURTHER RESOURCES

- *Prayer Shield* by C. Peter Wagner (Ventura, Calif.: Regal Books, 1992). This is my complete book about the subject of personal intercession and the gift of intercession. If you are an intercessor not yet strongly related to your pastor, I suggest you give your pastor a copy. If you are a pastor forming a team of intercessors, each one should have this book.

- *Partners in Prayer* by John Maxwell (Nashville: Thomas Nelson Publishers, 1996). This book contains practical wisdom from a leading pastor who has pioneered the prayer partner ministry in a local church.

- *The Pastor's Prayer Partners* by John Maxwell (Injoy Ministries, P.O. Box 19900, San Diego, CA 92159, 1-800-333-6506). This is the Cadillac of resources for developing personal prayer partners. It includes a videotape, six audiotapes and printed outlines for following each lesson. Call to order.

- *Preyed On or Prayed For* by Terry Teykl (Anderson, Ind.: Bristol Books, 1994). This book contains good insights and advice for recruiting prayer partners from one who is both a hands-on pastor and one of America's great contemporary prayer leaders.
- *Beyond the Veil: God's Call to Intimate Intercession* (1996) by Alice Smith (SpiriTruth Publishing, 7710-T Cherry Park Drive, Suite 224, Houston, TX 77095). This is the best book for understanding how gifted intercessors think and feel and pray.

Praying for Our Cities

I BELIEVE THAT THE CITIES OF THE WORLD HAVE BECOME the primary target for planning evangelistic strategy as we move into the twenty-first century. Other targets are legitimate as well. Dawn Ministries, for example, develops strategies for "Discipling A Whole Nation." The Joshua Project 2000, growing out of the A.D. 2000 Movement, has targeted 1,739 significant unreached people groups. Campus Crusade has chosen "Million People Target Areas" as its primary focus. Whatever unit we select, however, almost invariably large numbers of those who make up the unit will be found in cities.

TEARING DOWN SPIRITUAL "SOUND BARRIERS"

How can we make certain the cities of our nation and of the world are open to receive the good news of Jesus

Christ? I like the way John DeVries of Mission 21 India puts it: "The devil has created 'sound barriers' around every city and every people group; spiritual sound barriers which can only be torn down through prayer. We can have the best methods, phenomenal sums of money, and dedicated workers, but none of these can tear down the demonic, spiritual walls which keep people from hearing the gospel. Only prayer is effective! And once prayer is answered and the walls come tumbling down, all that remains is the 'mop up' operation, much like Israel's taking of Jericho."[1]

DeVries illustrates his point by citing a case study from Goa, the Portuguese-speaking, Roman Catholic city on the western shores of India. Goa had gained a reputation among Christian leaders in the whole region as being notoriously resistant to the gospel, according to S. Joseph, pastor of the New Life Fellowship in Bombay. In 1989, Pastor Joseph had gone to Goa to help plant churches, but, like others before him, he was stoned and run out of the city. Church-planting teams continued as well as they could, but after years of fighting a strenuous uphill battle they could only count six tiny, struggling house churches as the fruit of their labor.

In 1994, however, a Christian prayer team arrived from Brazil. These intercessors had been called to do a one-year prayer journey on behalf of the city of Goa. They rented a house and for 12 months did nothing but pray for the city. Then, having accomplished their assignment, they went back to Brazil. Did this do any good? Were their prayers of the powerful kind? Yes, they were. Pastor Joseph reported that in the two months following the departure of the Brazilian intercessors, his New Life movement had planted 18 new house churches!

Few people would expect to be assigned a one-year prayer journey for a single city on the other side of the world. However, rapidly increasing numbers of believers on every continent, some having the gift of intercession and some not having it, are moving outside of their churches to pray aggressively in their communities. They understand warfare prayer and know how it can penetrate those sound barriers of darkness so that the light of the gospel can shine through.

HOW REVIVAL WILL COME

As this extraordinary decade of the 1990s was just beginning, I heard what I take to be a prophetic word from a Southern Baptist pastor, Jack Graham of Prestonwood Baptist Church in Dallas, Texas. Speaking to a room full of younger pastors, he said: *"Revival will come when we get the walls down between the church and the community."* I have repeated this hundreds of times to tens of thousands of leaders since I first heard it.

I have also sensed that God is revealing a prophetic Scripture to accompany this admonition: namely, Joshua 1:3. The word from God to Joshua provided a literal mandate for his task of taking possession of the Promised Land: "Every place that the sole of your foot will tread upon I have given you."

Joshua's role was simply to put his physical body on the site, and then allow God to do the rest by using His supernatural power. He saw it demonstrated soon afterward when Jericho fell. By "prophetic Scripture" I mean that God, from time to time, seems to take a Scripture that may have had its own particular meaning in its own context perhaps thousands of years ago and brings it to life once again, just as literally as before, into another more contemporary context. This is how I view Joshua 1:3 for the 1990s and beyond. God is giving us new tools for action at this time of the final thrust for world evangelization, which I detailed in chapter 5. It is up to us to hear what the Spirit is saying to the churches, and once we hear it to decide that we will obey.

If we want to have our communities transformed by the power of God we must, therefore, pull down the walls. We must place the soles of our feet out into the community itself by employing our principal weapon of spiritual warfare: namely, prayer. This does not mean in any way that we should pray less inside our churches. A review of chapter 6 will be reminder enough that I feel strongly about local churches becoming true houses of prayer. We need to pray more inside our churches. We also need to pray more inside our homes. That is not all, though. We must also move outside of our churches by beseeching powerful prayer for our communities.

In theory, the power of prayer knows no boundaries or geographical limitations. This is true; but it is not the whole story. Other things being equal, on-site prayer is almost always more effective than distant prayer. Those who have a healing ministry know from experience that the same principle applies. Prayers for healing are answered for individuals in other states or in other countries.

Something about physical proximity, the laying on of hands, the anointing with oil and ministering one-on-one measurably increases the frequency of actual healings. It is by no means certain, for example, that the dramatic change in the spiritual atmosphere of the city of Goa would have taken place if the Brazilian prayer team would have stayed home and prayed for Goa from their homes or churches in Brazil.

PRAYER EVANGELISM

It is biblical to pray for the lost. Paul commissions Timothy to engage in spiritual warfare. He says, "This charge I commit to you, son Timothy, according to the prophecies previously made concerning you, that by them you may wage the good warfare" (1 Tim. 1:18). Paul's charge to Timothy emerges from the premise that "Christ Jesus came into the world to save sinners" (v. 15). Jesus came for so many other good things, though, that we at times forget His *primary* purpose: to save lost souls (see Luke 19:10).

The division in 1 Timothy between chapters 1 and 2 has often blocked us from seeing exactly what Paul's charge to Timothy focused on: namely, prayer. "Therefore," says Paul, "I exhort first of all that supplications, prayers, intercessions, and

---

> *"Prayer is the most tangible trace of eternity in the human heart. Intercessory prayer on behalf of the felt needs of the lost is the best way to open their eyes to the light of the gospel."*

---

giving of thanks be made for all men" (2:1). Why? Because "[God] desires all men to be saved and to come to the knowledge of the truth" (v. 4).

In the process of evangelism, bringing lost people from the power of Satan to God (see Acts 26:18), Paul recommends prayer *first of all.* Ed Silvoso believes this so strongly that he has introduced a new term into the English language: "prayer evangelism." In his outstanding book *That None Should Perish* (Regal Books), he begins each chapter with a principle. The principle underlying his chapter "Prayer Evangelism" states: *"Prayer is the most tangible trace of eternity in the human heart. Intercessory prayer on behalf of the felt needs of the lost is the best way to open their eyes to the light of the gospel"* (italics his).[2]

Ed Silvoso takes Paul's charge to Timothy literally when the only specific persons mentioned by Paul after telling Timothy to pray for "all men" is "for kings and all who are in authority" (1 Tim. 2:2). Silvoso suggests that this implies much more than just mentioning their names in prayer.

Silvoso says, "To pray effectively for them, it is necessary to go beyond this first step. We should go to those in authority and ask what their prayer requests are....The openness of the lost to intercessory prayer on their behalf has been the greatest surprise I have encountered in our city-reaching ministry. I have yet to be turned down by *anyone* in authority to whom prayer has been offered."[3] Could it be that personalized prayer for the public officials of our community might make a difference?

It seemed to work in Boulder, Colorado, according to an item in the *National and International Religion Report*. Boulder, a hub of witchcraft, satanic worship, New Age and the largest Buddhist temple in America, is now in the beginning stages of a Christian renewal. It seemed for a while as if the forces of darkness had the upper hand. Nearly half the churches in the county were experiencing serious divisions. Pastors were frustrated, angry and on the verge of leaving town. God, however, used a Nigerian graduate student to bring the pastors together for a weekly prayer meeting. Prayer began to change things in the city.

What happened? The first thing was that the pastors found their attitude toward the city changing. Mark Tidd, pastor of Crestview Christian Reformed Church, says that pastors who had been "praying as if Boulder was Sodom" began seeing the city "as Nineveh—more in need of compassion than condemnation." Then they did what Silvoso also advocates: they introduced themselves personally to Boulder's leaders—the mayor, city council members, county commissioners, chief of police, county sheriff, school leaders and others. When the authorities saw that the pastors genuinely wanted to serve them, the civic leaders were both shocked and delighted. Strong relationships formed, and the Christian community in Boulder began to get a fair hearing. Churches began to grow instead of fight. Tidd's congregation, for example, has more than doubled in four years.[4]

PASTORS AND INTERCESSORS IN HARMONY

In one of the books in *The Prayer Warrior Series—Warfare Prayer*—I include a chapter about the rules for praying for a city (see pages 161-178). I believe it would be helpful to reiterate two of the rules here and show how they relate to each other. A major starting point in encouraging changes in Boulder was the willingness of the pastors to meet together regularly to pray.

My rule goes like this: *Secure the unity of the pastors and other Christian leaders in the area and begin to pray together on a regular basis.* At this point, I am not advocating more ministerial or formal associations of churches. I am suggesting the *spiritual* unity that can come through praying together. It is important for the believers of a city to pray together, but it is much more crucial for the pastors to do it.

The reason for this is that the pastors are the divinely designated spiritual gatekeepers of a given city. I realize we have not thought too much about this in the past, and, in my opinion, this is a central reason many of our cities have been just like Boulder—a playground for the devil. When I use the term "spiritual gatekeepers," I am mainly raising the issue of authority. When it comes right down to it, no spiritual authority in a given city is higher than the pastors of the local churches. Even in cities where high-visibility leaders may head national and international parachurch ministries, those individuals rarely sense or exercise spiritual authority for the city in which they live. When the gatekeepers link together in one accord, however, the realm of darkness then becomes seriously threatened.

No one has done more in recent years than Francis Frangipane in catalyzing the unity of pastors in city after city. His book *The House of the Lord* (Creation House) is a classic. In it, he defines the house of the Lord as "that living, united, praying church in the city. The Lord's house will consist of evangelicals and Pentecostals, traditional churches and charismatics; it will be free of racial and class prejudices. They will simply be Christians who know Jesus as Lord, believe the truth of the Scriptures and are committed to one another as brethren."[5]

Here is how my friend Morris Cerullo views it: "Satan's number one goal in citywide warfare is to destroy the unity among the churches in that city. He will try to divide the leadership

---

It is helpful to see pastors as the hands and intercessors as the eyes. Whenever the hand reaches out to touch or grasp something to do a job, the eye guides the hand to the proper place.

---

with jealousy, competition and gossip. Then, he will try to divide church members of different churches one against the other. When the church is in disarray because of disunity, Satan moves his forces into the city promoting sin, corruption and a general oppression over the city and the churches of the city to keep the church from mounting a counterattack."[6]

THE CRUCIAL ROLE OF THE INTERCESSORS

This leads me to my second pertinent rule: *Work with intercessors especially gifted and called to strategic-level warfare, seeking God's revelation of: (a) the redemptive gift or gifts of the city; (b) Satan's strongholds in the city; (c) territorial spirits assigned to the city; (d) corporate sin past and present that needs to be dealt with; and (e) God's plan of attack and timing.*

Pastors praying together for their city is an essential starting point. If they do not move on to relate to the intercessors in a meaningful way, though, they are going into the battle with one hand tied behind their backs. Although there are exceptions here and there, few pastors have the gift of intercession. In the Body of Christ, the hand cannot say to the eye, "I have no need of you" (see 1 Cor. 12:21).

In this analogy, it is helpful to see pastors as the hands and intercessors as the eyes. Whenever the hand reaches out to touch or grasp something to do a job, the eye guides the hand to the proper place. In the more advanced stages of prayer for a city, "especially gifted and called" intercessors are recommended. In the last chapter, I stressed the importance of pastors of local churches connecting with personal intercessors.

As readers of *Prayer Shield* know, I have found it helpful to distinguish between general intercessors, crisis intercessors, personal intercessors and warfare intercessors. Although many intercessors minister across the board or in more than one area, some tend to feel called especially to one of them. At this point, the experienced warfare intercessors are the most effective.

What do the intercessors, teamed with the pastors, do? Here is where much of the content of this book comes together. The intercessors are familiar with strategic-level intercession (chapter 3), so they see the whole picture from the perspective of the invisible world. Through spiritual mapping (chapter 4), they discern the principal targets, both positive and negative, toward which prayer needs to be focused. They understand identificational repentance (chapter 5) and know where to look for the corporate sin that needs to be remitted. They are especially gifted to hear from God (chapter 2), and know His direction for timing and procedure.

The intercessors, however, do not make the final decisions of what should be done and when. They are under the authority of the pastors who discern the proper application of what they hear through the intercessors. Sensitive intercessors will never yield to the temptation of attempting to control the pastors either by personal persuasion or through spiritual means. When they appear to appropriate authority to themselves, the relationship with pastors frequently breaks down.

Working together in harmony, city pastors and city intercessors are an unbeatable combination. Satan knows this well, and he knows it better than do many Christian leaders. The Bible tells us not to be ignorant of Satan's devices (see 2 Cor. 2:11). Two of his most used and most effective devices for blinding the minds of lost people in a city or in a nation to the glories of the gospel of Christ are (1) keeping the pastors of the city apart from each other, and (2) keeping the pastors and the intercessors from building strong relationships. If Satan or the principalities of darkness assigned to a specific city can succeed in doing this, they are home free. They can use the city for their playground and steal, kill and destroy almost at will.

DOES THIS WORK? LOOK AT GOIANIA, BRAZIL

Ed Silvoso not only writes books about prayer evangelism in cities, but he also practices it. I happened to be working with him at a conference in Los Angeles awhile ago at which five women who flew in from Goiania, Brazil, introduced themselves as intercessors. They invited Ed to minister in their city, and he said he would, but they must first talk to the city pastors when they arrived back home.

In Latin America—the *macho* culture—women usually do not take the initiative in projects of significance, and when they attempt it, the men more than likely head in the other direction. Still, the intercessors called the city pastors to a meeting. Silvoso tells what happened: "Usually pastors do not respond to impromptu invitations even when important pastors send them, *much less when they come from three unknown housewives.* The odds against these ladies succeeding were enormous. How many pastors showed up? Over 120. Incredible! A true miracle!"[7]

The intercessors were bold enough to suggest to the pastors that it might be God's timing for a new move ahead in their city and they also admitted they had gone ahead and tentatively invited Ed Silvoso to conduct a training seminar about prayer evangelism. The anointing of God must have been powerful because the pastors thought it was a good idea and became enthusiastic about it. Furthermore, instead of taking control of what was shaping up to be a major event, as would have been expected, they commissioned the intercessors to move ahead, promising their full support, and laying hands on the women to receive the power of the Holy Spirit for their job.

The next week, the women launched a radio program and soon had more than 100,000 people in the area praying together with them on the radio for one-and-a-half hours every day. Before long, nearly everyone in that large city of more than 1 million, including the city officials, knew about the intercessors and their huge prayer team.

THE PRISON RIOT: CALL THE INTERCESSORS!

Just three weeks before Ed Silvoso arrived for his prayer evangelism seminar, a riot broke out in the Goiania prison. The rebellious inmates took two judges, a chaplain, many guards and others hostage. They set entire cell blocks on fire. After several days of violent confrontation, they threatened to kill the hostages. The situation had reached a crisis. The governor of the state had sent his best troops, but they could not penetrate the prison.

As Silvoso tells it, "[The governor] chose better and more powerful weapons. Having heard about the praying ladies, he called them. When the ladies, together with several pastors, showed up at the governor's palace, with tears streaming down his cheeks, he told them, 'My weapons are useless for the emergency I am facing. I need a better weapon and you have it: prayer. Can you take over and bring resolution to this major crisis?'"[8]

The intercessors were not surprised. They had been praying, along with 100,000 others, for the city in the midst of crisis. They practiced two-way prayer and received a clear enough word from the Lord to say to the governor, "Do not worry anymore. Within 24 hours everything will be resolved with no bloodshed!" The governor then turned over his cellular phone, which had a hot line to the army colonel in charge of the government troops, instructing the colonel to take whatever action the ladies indicated, because they were hearing what the Holy Spirit had to say.

The result? Ed Silvoso reports, "Before the 24 hours were over the inmates surrendered, all the hostages were released, the two judges as well as many guards received the Lord, and the ladies were publicly honored by the governor for having resolved an impossible situation. Now the governor's palace is wide open for prayer meetings and a city of over one million people knows that God cares!"[9]

I visited Goiania a few months later, and I have seen firsthand how the harmony between pastors and intercessors has opened the spiritual atmosphere over the city for the rapid advance of the kingdom of God.

HOW TO GET STARTED

It is hard to read about these examples of praying in the community without saying, "I wish that could happen in my city as well!" It probably can. Maybe it is. The fact of the matter is that a majority of our larger cities in the United States now have citywide prayer movements at some stage of development.

For years in my prayer seminars, a few folks have raised their hands when I asked if the pastors in their city were meeting for prayer on some kind of a regular basis. I am amazed at how rapidly the proportion of hands has escalated in only the last couple of years or so. I realize it is not scientific, but it has led me to believe that at this writing about half of America's cities have started some kind of prayer movement. At this rate of increase, it will not be long before the city that does not have a citywide prayer movement will be an exception to the rule.

Several years of cumulative experience have surfaced a number of attractive ways of praying for a community, most of them well within reach of existing churches, pastors, intercessors and prayer ministries. Although it is not possible to include them all in this chapter, I will briefly highlight those I consider to have shown above average potential for across-the-board application.

Begin with the Right Heart and the Right Attitude

It is necessary to recognize from the start, and never forget, that the source of power for reaching a city is God, and that knowing His direction and timing is crucial. Intimacy with God is a nonnegotiable. Whether you are an intercessor or not, if you want to begin praying for your city, I recommend that you read Alice Smith's *Beyond the Veil*, which many regard as the best current book about intimacy with God.

For example, Bobbye Byerly, one of Doris's and my closest personal intercessors and U.S. National Board President of Women's Aglow Fellowship International, says, "Alice so skillfully weaves the depth of God's call, plus the deep yearning within intercessors to respond and seek His face. I could not put it down. I believe the holy call that is coming forth for intimacy is more clearly reached here than in anything else I've read."[10]

The following is the kind of statement you will find in the book: "The door of intimacy is open to all those who will enter. The Lord delights in the believer who, yearning to know what cannot be known naturally, enters the throne room through prayer with simplicity and humility. Beyond this veil, the child of God will touch the heart of God, bask in His loving words of affirmation, tremble at His unlimited power and authority, and come away forever changed."[11] I highly recommend this book for all who are serious in reaching their cities for God.

Be sure to allow God access to your own heart. Cleanse any strongholds that might invite spiritual forces to enter. Be sure you have no unconfessed sin. If you seem to be subject to irresistible temptations, find someone to pray for you or deliver you. If you fail to do this, you will open yourself to becoming a vulnerable target for a possible counterattack of the forces of evil.

Double check the authority issue. Do you have or are you working under the covering of sufficient spiritual authority to move into your city or target area? Are the spiritual gatekeepers in agreement? In most cases, it is unrealistic to expect 100 percent agreement, so it is best to discern whether a sufficient number of pastors of life-giving churches are involved in this effort. If the leaders are not in agreement, the timing may not be right.

Francis Frangipane says, "We also want to remove any sense of human pressure concerning citywide prayer....To seek to motivate pastors by pressure or manipulation will only breed resentment among them; they will fail to find the sweet pleasure which comes when leaders willingly seek God together."[12]

Finally, reexamine your motives. Be sure your attitudes about praying for your city are totally in line with the fruit of the Spirit (see Gal. 5:22,23). If you have any feelings of getting even with someone, of finger pointing, of resentment, of self-righteousness or of carnal pleasure in having the judgment of God fall on perceived "bad guys," work on that by covering the multitude of sins with love. If you can do that, you are ready for war.

A Twenty-Four-Hour Prayer Vigil

Concerts of Prayer International, led by David Bryant, helped catalyze a massive prayer effort in New York City, which is producing tangible results. First of all, several pastors of the city gathered for prayer and issued the Metro New York City Prayer Covenant, agreeing to uphold their city in prayer. Concerts of Prayer personnel from their Urban Strategies Division came alongside the pastors and agreed to mobilize as many churches as possible to participate in what is called "The Lord's Watch." The Lord's Watch is a multiethnic, ongoing, 24-hour-a-day prayer vigil for revival, reconciliation, reformation and reaching the lost. They keep intercessors linked by distributing a newsletter published in English, Spanish and Korean.

Each participating church chooses one day a month, and on that day every month it agrees to cover the city for 24 hours. By using this plan, as few as 31 churches could make sure that their city is being prayed for every hour of every day. New York, though, has more than 31 churches participating; it has no fewer than 130. The city is being prayed for at all times, not just by one church, but by four or five. Many of the churches have more than 100 of their members participating. The goal of The Lord's Watch is eventually to have 1,000 churches actively on board.

You might think this quantity of prayer would make a difference in the city. All the results are not yet in, but one of the most encouraging signs has been a marked decrease in New York City's crime rates every year for the past three years. The elated police department is predicting that if this trend continues, crime will drop below levels not experienced since 1968, when John V. Lindsay was mayor and a subway token cost 20 cents! Sociologists might speculate on other explanations, but the pastors of the city are absolutely convinced that this is a direct result of the massive citywide prayer during the last few years. Major advances have also been recorded in Christian unity and racial reconciliation within the city.

A variation on this, called The Watchman Prayer Alert, was conceived by Larry Thompson, a Southern Baptist pastor. First developed to cover a local church in prayer, it has expanded to cities. The week is divided into 168 hour-long periods. Church prayer groups from participating churches choose one or more of the hours of the week, and agree to pray together for the city during that hour. When one group is finishing its hour, it calls a representative of the group committed to the next hour, and so on to build a level of accountability. If a group fails to respond for two consecutive weeks, a discussion is held with the city prayer coordinator, and if it happens again the group is dropped. This latter program obviously demands a higher commitment than does The Lord's Watch, but either of them will provide a substantial prayer covering for the city.

Marches for Jesus

In 1996 more than 170 nations of the world, including 625 cities in the United States, participated in Marches for Jesus. An estimated 10 million believers, spanning every time zone, were marching in the streets of more than 2,000 cities on May 25, 1996.

This success was far beyond the wildest dreams of the four creative leaders, Graham Kendrick, Roger Forster, Gerald Coates and Lynn Green. They decided to get the walls down between the churches and the community in London in 1985 and place the soles of their feet out on the streets of London's notorious Soho district. They first used the name "March for Jesus" in 1987, and 15,000 went out into the streets of London singing praises to the King of kings. Graham Kendrick says the idea emerged when he "became interested in the dynamics of praise and in its relation to prayer and spiritual warfare."[13]

For the churches of many cities, the March for Jesus has become as much of a permanent part of their calendars as have Christmas and Easter. In Sao Paulo, Brazil, some 1.2 million marched this year and received coverage on every national Brazilian television network. Governor Pataki of New York and

Governor Wilson of California each issued official "March for Jesus Day" proclamations.

In Guatemala City, 100,000 marched, breaking the record for any public march in history. Tonga, just west of the international date line, held the first march of the day, led by the

---

"Defined prayerwalking is praying on-site with insight. It is simply praying in the very places that we expect God to bring forth His answers."

---

king and queen no less, who later hosted a banquet for the participants. In Pittsburgh, Pennsylvania, one of the police officers assigned to the march donated his day's paycheck to help pay the bills.

If your city did not have a March for Jesus this year, plan one next year. Help is available when you register at one of the offices listed in the resource section at the end of this chapter. It will make a difference in your city.

Prayerwalking

A 24-hour prayer vigil or a March for Jesus require some degree of citywide organization. Prayerwalking, however, can be simple, and it is the most feasible way to get started for many who say, "Yes, I want to get the walls down and put the soles of my feet in my community with prayer." Next week, if you want to, you can get together with one or two Christian friends in your neighborhood, simply walk the streets of your neighborhood and pray for a half hour or 45 minutes. Pray for the families in the homes you pass; pray for the schools; pray for those who drive by; pray for the businesses; pray for the police officers. Be open to God so He can indicate directly to you for what you should be praying.

Steve Hawthorne, arguably today's apostle for prayerwalking, describes it as follows: "God is rousing Christians to pray for their cities in an 'up close and personal' way. Christians are pressing their prayers beyond the walls of church buildings to bring clear and quiet blessing on their neighbors in Jesus' name....This sort of on-site intercession has come to be called 'prayerwalking.' Defined prayerwalking is praying on-site with insight. It is simply praying in the very places that we expect God to bring forth His answers."[14]

According to Hawthorne, three basic models of prayerwalking have surfaced:

1. **Home Zone** prayerwalking is where Christians prayerwalk where they live, work, study, worship or play. The model I mentioned in the paragraph before last would fit here.
2. **Key Site** prayerwalking involves selecting a certain place or several places and targeting them for special, sustained prayer focus. Identifying such places is a function of spiritual mapping.
3. **Total Coverage** prayerwalking aims to cover the entire city in prayerwalking in a systematic and ongoing fashion. Hawthorne has a remarkable vision for what he calls "PrayerWalk USA" in which every home on every street in the country will be prayed for regularly by the year 2000. He is monitoring the progress by zip code.[15]

Neighborhood Houses of Prayer
Neighborhood Houses of Prayer, developed by my friends John DeVries and Alvin Vander Griend, also aim to cover each neighborhood in prayer, but the design is slightly more formal and

organized than general prayerwalking. Church leaders who are more comfortable with structure will welcome so-called Houses of Prayer.

A premise underlying Houses of Prayer, in John DeVries's words, is: "There's a territorial aspect to prayer. We do not merely pray for individuals, but we pray for households, neighborhoods, businesses and communities."[16] In this plan, backed by excellent start-up resources, a group of believers decide to meet together in a certain place such as a home, a dorm or a business for prayer once a week. This meeting is called a House of Prayer, and the group can order an "official" flag to hang on the porch or some other convenient place.

The weekly meeting is held inside, but during the following week the members are assigned to pray on site for certain groups of houses or other targets. As the group members do this, they attempt to make contacts or build relationships with the individuals for whom they are praying. They offer to pray for people's specific needs in the weekly House of Prayer meeting. If the people are not home, door hangers invite them to call a number and share their prayer requests. They have established a wide-open feedback channel to receive and record specific details of answered prayers in the neighborhood.

If it is true that revival will come when we get the walls down between the church and the community, the wonderfully varied ways and means God is giving us to pray in our communities must lead us to believe that revival is close at hand.

■ REFLECTION QUESTIONS ■

1. Just as a rough estimate, what percentage of Christian prayer in your city do you think is done in the community as

opposed to in churches or in homes? What percentage should it be?

2. You may not have heard the term "prayer evangelism" before reading this chapter. Describe it in your own words.

3. To your knowledge, what is being done among the pastors of your city by way of encouraging a citywide prayer movement?

4. Have you ever prayerwalked? If not, would you be inclined to begin? What would it take to get regular prayerwalking spread through your city?

Notes

1. John DeVries, personal report to the author, 1995.
2. Ed Silvoso, *That None Should Perish* (Ventura, Calif.: Regal Books, 1994), p. 57.
3. Ibid., p. 73.
4. *National and International Religion Report* (September 4, 1995).
5. Francis Frangipane, *The House of the Lord* (Lake Mary, Fla.: Creation House, 1991), pp. 11-12.
6. Morris Cerullo, "Spiritual Warfare Prayer," *Victory Miracle Living* (August 1996): 32.
7. Ed Silvoso, circular letter dated June 17, 1996.
8. Ibid.
9. Ibid.
10. Bobbye Byerly's endorsement inside the front cover of *Beyond the Veil* by Alice Smith (Houston: SpiriTruth Publishing, 1996).
11. Ibid., p. 13.
12. Frangipane, *The House of the Lord,* p. 94.
13. Graham Kendrick, Gerald Coates, Roger Forster and Lynn Green, *March for Jesus* (Eastbourne, England: Kingsway Publications Ltd., 1992), p. 24.
14. Steve Hawthorne, *PrayerWalk Organizer Guide* (Austin, Tex.: PrayerWalk USA, 1996), p. 9.
15. These terms and concepts are taken from the *PrayerWalk Organizer Guide.*
16. John DeVries, *What Is a Neighborhood House of Prayer?* (Grand Rapids: Neighborhood Houses of Prayer, n.d.), p. 3.

FURTHER RESOURCES

- *Warfare Prayer* by C. Peter Wagner (Ventura, Calif.: Regal Books, 1992). Check the chapter "The Rules for City Taking."
- *That None Should Perish* by Ed Silvoso (Ventura, Calif.:

Regal Books, 1994). This book provides a powerful explanation of prayer evangelism. It is the one book on this list I would make required reading.

- *Taking Your Cities for God* by John Dawson (Orlando, Fla.: Creation House, 1989). This book is now considered a classic about praying for cities.
- *Commitment to Conquer* by Bob Beckett (Grand Rapids: Chosen Books, 1997). This book is full of stimulating insights about how to minister to a city. It is written by a local church pastor who has seen remarkable results.
- *Prayerwalking* by Steve Hawthorne and Graham Kendrick (Orlando, Fla.: Creation House, 1993). This book is a practical guide for how to move out in prayer "on site with insight."
- *The House of the Lord* by Francis Frangipane (Orlando, Fla.: Creation House, 1991). Guidelines for bringing together the pastors of a city on the premise that it takes a citywide church to win a citywide war.
- *Neighborhood Houses of Prayer* by John DeVries and Alvin Vander Griend (Mission 21 India, P.O. Box 141312, Grand Rapids, MI 49514). A complete package including two videotapes to get you and your church started in organizing neighborhood houses of prayer. Order from the above address.
- The two offices for the March for Jesus are located in the following areas: In the United States and the Americas, write to March for Jesus, USA, P.O. Box 3216, Austin, TX 78764. For the rest of the world write to Global March for Jesus, P.O. Box 39, Sunbury-on-Thames, Middlesex TW 16 6PP, England, U.K.

Prayer Power for the Nations

T HE WA ARE A WARLIKE PEOPLE GROUP OF 3 MILLION located in the northeast part of Myanmar (Burma), on the Chinese border. They are very independent and they refuse to submit to the Myanmar government, which itself is one of the most repressive governments on earth at the present time. Myanmar has sent some of its crack troops to subdue the Wa, but they have consistently been forced to retreat.

ONE HUNDRED BAPTISMS
FOR ONE HUNDRED HEADS

Not long ago, the government attempted to calm down the Wa by sending them a gift of some statues of Buddha. Much to the surprise and consternation of the authorities, the Wa returned the presents immediately, and asked that the statues be replaced by 100 Bibles and some Christian missionaries! They said they wanted to know more about God.

Some Burmese missionaries were able to go and minister to the Wa, and soon the chief, a headhunter, was saved. His baptism proved to be one of a kind. After he was immersed in the name of the Father, Son and Holy Spirit, he then commenced to duck himself under the water 100 more times—one for every human head he had taken during his nefarious career! He then volunteered to become a speaker for the *Jesus* film team that was evangelizing the region![1]

How could such an amazing thing have happened? Human explanations fall short. Only the hand of God could have brought about such a change. Based on what has been said in virtually every chapter of this book, prayer, more than anything else, is the spiritual force that releases the hand of God. Myanmar, including its cities and people groups, has never been prayed for so much as right now, and both the quantity and the quality of prayer on behalf of Myanmar and its people groups are escalating so rapidly that no one can keep up with it.

That wonderful incident adds the Wa as one more stanza to the "new song" the 24 elders and the four living creatures will sing to the Lamb on the throne: "[You] have redeemed us to God by Your blood out of every tribe and tongue and people and nation" (Rev. 5:9). This song cannot be sung quite yet because many more nations, tribes and peoples still need salvation. However, I believe in the motto of the A.D. 2000 Movement, which states: "A church for every people and the gospel for every person by the year 2000." The number of the significantly large (more than 10,000) and least-reached people groups at this writing is 1,739, most of them located in the 10/40 Window, the geographical area from 10° to 40° north of the equator, as shown in the following diagram:

"10/40 WINDOW"

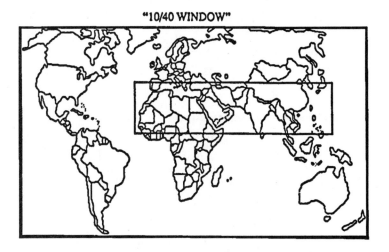

CAN OUR GENERATION COMPLETE THE GREAT COMMISSION?

Right now, a baby born in most places inside the 10/40 Window will have no reasonable opportunity to hear the gospel of Jesus Christ in his or her lifetime. I believe that by the end of the year 2000, however, every baby born any place in the world will have a reasonable opportunity to hear the gospel in his or her lifetime. As I mentioned in chapter 5, this is the first time in human history that we have a viable opportunity of completing the Great Commission of Jesus in our generation. By this, I do not mean everyone in the world will be saved. I do mean, however, to paraphrase the words of Jesus, "this gospel of the kingdom will have been preached in all the world as a witness to all the nations" (see Matt. 24:14).

Modestly claiming some credentials of a professional missiologist, including specialization in strategies of missions and evangelism, let me hasten to say that no known human missiological or evangelistic strategy could be designed to accomplish such a task. Only the sovereign God, through the most awesome outpouring of supernatural power ever imagined, could make this happen. Just as in the case of the Wa of Myanmar, so the almighty hand of God must be released if we are going to see the vision of A.D. 2000 materialize. There is no other way!

What is it that moves the hand of God to redeem the nations? Apparently it is prayer—the prayers of the saints.

Back to the 24 elders and the four living creatures around the throne. Scripture says that each one of them had, besides a harp, "golden bowls full of incense, which are *the prayers of the saints*" (Rev. 5:8, emphasis mine). What is it that moves the hand of God to redeem the nations? Apparently it is prayer—the prayers of the saints. I realize there are few exegetical grounds for doing this, but could I be pardoned for expanding this vision a bit and imagining that there could be a golden bowl for each one of the world's people groups? If so, we might surmise that the bowls for the unreached people groups are not yet full.

The metaphor of the incense being the prayers of the saints is mentioned again in Revelation 8:3,4, where it adds that fire from God's altar is added and amazing things happen on earth (see Rev. 8:5). Dutch Sheets says, "According to these verses, either when [God] knows it is the right time to do something or when enough prayer has accumulated to get the job done, He releases power. He takes the bowl and mixes it with fire from the altar."[2]

Filling the Golden Bowls
If this is the case, and if the real situation is at least *something* like that, it follows that the most crucial missiological activity at

the moment is to fill those bowls as quickly as possible. It is essential that the prayers of the saints be mobilized as they never have been before to complete the Great Commission in our lifetime. For several years my wife, Doris, and I have been deeply engaged in that effort. We feel privileged to have been entrusted with the coordination of the United Prayer Track of the A.D. 2000 Movement, and we are amazed at how prayer actually is being mobilized on every continent.

I would not be surprised if the year 1990 will eventually be looked upon as a hinge year in the history of the Christian movement. As I have previously indicated, in this decade we are seeing the greatest harvest of souls ever known, the greatest outward manifestation of spiritual power, the greatest Christian unity in 1,600 years, the greatest influence of the Third World in Christian affairs and the greatest worldwide prayer movement. Little of what we are seeing now was being predicted with any degree of accuracy or recognition in the 1980s or prior to that.

Our task of mobilizing prayer for world evangelization is easier now than it ever could have been in the past. We look at our job as not to get people praying—God is doing that in the most amazing ways—but our job is to get praying people. We attempt to put the intercessors and the prayer ministries of the world in touch with each other and get them praying in "one accord," as it says in Acts 1:14. It has occurred to me that if Luke thought it significant enough to record in Acts 1 that 120 individuals were praying in one accord, what would he think if he knew we are now getting 120 *nations* to pray together in one accord? But it is happening!

HYPOTHESIS: THE MORE PRAYER THE BETTER

My hypothesis is that the more prayer the better. The Bible teaches about the benefits of agreement in prayer in several places. Jesus said, "Where two or three are gathered together in My name, I am there in the midst of them" (Matt. 18:20). By this I do not mean one person praying alone has no value or does no good. I am saying, though, that when two or more agree in prayer, it is incrementally more powerful than just one person praying.

We read in the Old Testament that if one can put 1,000 to flight, two can put 10,000 to flight (see Deut. 32:30). I heard

---

Some kind of exponential increase in the power of prayer occurs when more people are praying together about the same thing.

---

that the winner of a horse-pull contest at a county fair pulled 9,000 pounds, and the runner-up pulled 8,000 pounds. Hitched together, though, the two horses pulled 25,000 pounds! Likewise, some kind of exponential increase in the power of prayer occurs when more people are praying together about the same thing.

I thought of this when I was in Colombia recently. I learned that in Cali, the vortex of the South American drug cartels, believers have come together for prayer in a magnitude and with a scheduled regularity I have not heard of in any other city. They rent the largest soccer stadium in Cali three times a year for all-night prayer meetings. In the last two meetings, 50,000 believers packed the stadium and thousands were turned away. You know that something extraordinary is happening when stadiums begin to be packed all night long just for prayer!

In Seoul, Korea, those numbers have been exceeded several times, although not on such a regularly scheduled basis. Certain events, however, have drawn more than 1 million to pray together in Yoido Plaza on two or three occasions. Up to 90,000 pack the new Olympic stadium for prayer meetings from time to time.

A MIGHTY ARMY OF PRAYER WARRIORS

The A.D. 2000 United Prayer Track has been moving in several parallel directions, not the least being the so-called "Praying Through the Window" initiative. In 1991, Luis Bush, International Director of the A.D. 2000 Movement, woke up in the middle of the night in Bangladesh and wrote a letter to me. The letter said, in part, "Peter, if we are to see a spiritual breakthrough and an advance of the Gospel so that the church is established in the 10/40 Window World by A.D. 2000, it is going to take an enormous prayer and fasting initiative. We need a mighty army of strategic-level prayer warriors saying: *Lord, give me the 10/40 Window or I'll die.* We need at least one million who are prepared to pray until breakthrough occurs."

Soon after that, a group consisting of Dick Eastman, Jane Hansen, Bobbye Byerly, Ted Haggard, Luis Bush, Doris Wagner and Alvin Low gathered in Colorado Springs to pray and seek God's direction. They boldly asked the question: "Might it be possible to do as Luis Bush suggests and mobilize one million Christians to pray in one accord for the nations and unreached peoples of the 10/40 Window?" Their response: "Why not? Let's go for it!" They thought at the time they were exercising great faith. Now they look back and say, in undisguised delight: "Oh, we of little faith!"

Praying Through the Window I, for example, focused prayers on the 62 nations (there are now 64) of the 10/40 Window. I want to emphasize that targeting our prayers toward these nations in no way is intended to make a statement that lost souls elsewhere in any part of the world do not need powerful prayer. Sweden needs prayer as much as Sri Lanka; Brazil needs prayer as much as Bangladesh; Toronto needs prayer as much as Tokyo; and the Navajo need prayer as much as the Nepali. The leaders of the A.D. 2000 Movement, however, believe that God is giving them a special mandate to focus primarily on the 10/40 Window until the end of the year 2000, when, by charter, the organization ceases to exist. Meanwhile, other movements are focusing on other parts of the world, and the Body of Christ is praying for the lost wherever they may be found.

During October 1993, not 1 million, but more than 21 million believers around the world prayed for the same two nations on the same day. They followed a prayer calendar that had been translated into many languages and distributed far and wide. Some said the prayer calendar could well have been the most duplicated piece of paper in the world during the whole year. Many people, particularly in China, were following the prayer calendar through daily radio broadcasts. It could well be that Praying Through the Window I set a record for the most Christians participating in a synchronized way in a global prayer effort.

SHAKING UP INDIA'S GOD OF GOOD LUCK

India was one of the two nations targeted for prayer the first day, October 1, 1993, and the nation was strongly affected. Apparently, on that day the prayers must have filled some golden bowl to which God added His "fire from the altar" (Rev. 8:5), for when this happens the Bible says there will be "noises, thunderings, lightnings, and an earthquake." I am not arguing that this prophecy was altogether literally fulfilled on October 1, 1993, but the parallel is fascinating, to say the least.

The following is the story of that day's earthquake in India from *Time* magazine:

> With the head of an elephant and the body of a pot-bellied man, Lord Ganesha is one of Hinduism's most beloved deities, a god of new beginnings and good luck. Multitudes of peasants in the hinterland reaches of Maharashtra, a western Indian state that is home to the god's most devout cult...were concluding a 10-day festival in Ganesha's honor celebrated late into the night with dancing, singing, and blowing horns. In Killari, a village of about 15,500 near the Karnataka state border, the ceremonies culminated in the ritual dipping of the god's idols in the village pond. Around 1 a.m., worshippers struggled home and fell into a deep slumber. It was a sleep from which most of them never awoke. At 3:56 a.m., an earthquake struck with a deafening roar and a rattling movement that swept across the southern sector of the Deccan Plateau.[3]

This was not a routine earthquake. The following year the Geological Society of India published a book about that earthquake, claiming it will go down in history as the deadliest earthquake ever to strike a stable continental region, occurring in a place long considered by geologists as being virtually immune to such shocks.

Professor B. E. Vijayam, a member of the Geological Society and a committed Christian believer who the previous year had won India's Scientist of the Year Award, was awakened by the shaking of his windows as he was sleeping in another state many miles away. Realizing at once that earthquakes should not be happening in this part of India, the Lord impressed on him Jesus' words that earthquakes in various places would be a sign of the end times. He located these words in Matthew

24:7, and read on to verse 14: "And this gospel of the kingdom will be preached in all the world as a witness to all nations, and then the end will come." This became a personal word from God to him to devote his life to seeing that every unreached people group of India be reached with the gospel. Little did he know that he became one of the answers to the prayers of 21 million Christians on the day of the earthquake.

That is not all. Up till that time, not much progress had been made in spreading the gospel in the state of Sikkim in northern India. On October 1, however, the spiritual forces keeping the Sikkim people in captivity seemed to weaken, and since then approximately 100 a day have been converted from Tibetan Buddhism. Reports claim that between 10 percent and 20 percent of the people in Sikkim are believers at this writing.

Dick Eastman, who was the cochairperson (along with Jane Hansen of Aglow International) of Praying Through the Window I, reports that his ministry, Every Home for Christ, was starting three new "Christ groups," many of which are embryonic churches, in India every day. They were happy with that kind of fruit. In the year following the October event, however, the number increased to as many as 17 Christ groups a day! Eastman knows of nothing else that could have caused the dramatic change other than 21 million people praying in one accord for India on October 1, 1993.

Praying Through the Window II was conceived in the extraordinary wave of faith following Praying Through the Window I. Michael Little, president of the Christian Broadcasting Network (CBN), agreed to chair the committee and the target became the 100 "Gateway Cities" of the 10/40 Window. These were not necessarily the 100 largest cities, but there was reason to believe they were among the most spiritually significant cities. Each of the nations had a minimum of one Gateway City on the list.

To help increase the number of those praying "in one accord," several high-quality resources were released. A prayer calendar, similar to the first one, featured three cities on some days and four on other days of October 1995. The worldwide circulation of that prayer calendar in many languages was amazing. One indication of this was a fascinating discovery made by a prayer journey team from New Life Church of Colorado Springs.

A LOCAL CHURCH CAN MAKE A DIFFERENCE

Pastor Ted Haggard of New Life Church is one of the most active of all local church pastors in leading and mobilizing his people to pray for the 10/40 Window. As a starter, he has suspended full-sized flags of every nation and territory in the world from the ceiling of the huge worship center. The flags of the 10/40 Window nations display identifying labels. Haggard is a member of the Praying Through the Window Committee, and his church also staffs and finances the Christian Information Network. This network has been assigned the immense task of coordinating all the prayer journeys into the 10/40 Window. In October 1993, Haggard led a team from his church to pray in Albania. As soon as they returned, he began seeking the Lord about where they should go in October 1995.

Ted Haggard is not one to shy away from formidable challenges. When the reports from Praying Through the Window I were released by Christian Information Network, only one of the 62 nations of the 10/40 Window had not been visited by a prayer journey team in 1993—Qatar, a small peninsula in the Arabian Gulf next to Saudi Arabia. That information was enough to prompt Ted to pray, "God, how about Qatar?" The answer was, "Go for it!"—or words to that effect.

Prayer in a Secret Meeting

Qatar is far from the easiest country to visit. Visas for Westerners are next to nonexistent. God opened the door, however, and a couple of days after Pastor Ted and his team arrived they were met by some expatriate secret believers. Invited to attend the clandestine meeting late one night, the team was led through what seemed to be mazes of streets and alleys until they came to an apparently empty building. Then passing through another maze of doors and corridors and stairways, they finally entered the dark meeting room. Only after the door was closed was a small light bulb turned on. The windows had been cemented shut so no noise could be heard outside.

You can imagine Pastor Ted's utter amazement when he saw a Praying Through the Window II Gateway Cities prayer calendar pasted on one wall! The believers had not made the connection that this prayer team from Colorado was somehow associated with the calendar. For all they knew, they were the only ones who had it and who were faithfully praying for the cities day by day! What incredible delight it was for them when they learned that millions of fellow believers in virtually every nation of the world were praying "in one accord" with them and for them!

Besides the prayer calendar, which appeared in such unexpected places, YWAM Publishing printed a 150-page book, *Praying Through the 100 Gateway Cities of the 10/40 Window.* The book contains a one-page profile of each city, including a map and significant prayer points for the city. Added to that, CBN produced a full-length video called *Light the World,* which was translated into several languages. Copies of the video were distributed and run in churches and on television stations around the world.

REPORTING THE ANSWERS: *WINDOWATCHMAN*

By October 1995, we had faith enough to expect that the 21 million Praying Through the Window I would be exceeded. So we were elated when Beverly Pegues, director of the Christian

Information Network, released the figure of more than 36 million praying for the Gateway Cities in one accord! The results of each of the first two Praying Through the Window initiatives are published in books edited by Pegues called *WindoWatchman* and *WindoWatchman II.* These books make an effort to report back to the intercessors and to the Body of Christ in general how their prayers have been answered.

Praying Through the Window III is underway as this volume is being written. The target is the 1,739 most significant yet unreached people groups of the 10/40 Window. The prayer calendar has grouped them into 146 "Gateway Clusters" for the 31 days of October 1997. A 120-page book, *The Unreached Peoples,* written and edited by The Caleb Project, has been released. It describes each cluster and includes maps of their locations for the days on which they will receive prayer.

A full-length video, *To the Ends of the Earth,* has been produced by CBN. Bethany World Prayer Center, a local church in Baton Rouge, Louisiana, pastored by Larry Stockstill, has undertaken the immense task of researching, writing and publishing four-page profiles of each of the 1,739 unreached people groups. Another local church, the Manna Church of Fayetteville, North Carolina, pastored by Michael Fletcher, has installed a new database and is in the process of enlisting 17,390 local churches, each of which will commit to pray fervently for an assigned people group, not just in 1997, but till the end of the year 2000. This means that each unreached people group will have no fewer than 10 congregations concentrating prayer on them week after week and month after month.

There is more. Bethany World Prayer Center, a top leader of the worldwide home-cell group movement, agreed to sign up 10 home-cell groups that would commit to pray for an assigned unreached people group through A.D. 2000. In less than a year this had been accomplished and, as of this writing, they are working on round two, now determined to have 20 home-cell groups praying for each of the 1,739 unreached people groups. This means that 34,780 groups will be helping to fill the golden bowls of the nations week after week and month after month.

I won't venture a guess of how many will participate in this third effort, but I will be surprised if it does not exceed our current expectations and dreams. The reason I am recording all these facts and figures is simply to build our faith that the prayers of the saints are, indeed, filling the golden bowls with incense. This pleases God and moves His hand to release nation after nation and people group after people group from the powers of darkness that have up till now managed to keep their minds blinded to the gospel.

PRAYER JOURNEYS

Let me repeat Jack Graham's quote from the last chapter: "Revival will come when we get the walls down between the church and the community." I mentioned there that two of the exciting new ways Christians are getting into their cities with prayer are through praise marches and prayerwalking.

Two other forms of prayer outside the churches could relate more to the category of praying for whole nations rather than for specific cities: namely, prayer journeys and prayer expeditions. In the reports about the Praying Through the Window initiatives, I mentioned "prayer journeys" several times, such as Ted Haggard's prayer journey to Qatar. These require a bit more explanation.

Each one of the prayer efforts combines millions of home-based and church-based pray-ers and also some who are called and equipped to go on prayer journeys in which they pray "on site with insight." Both of them are important if we are going to pray seriously and powerfully for the nations. In *WindoWatchman,* for example, Beverly Pegues shows how they fit together:

As you read about [the prayer journeyers'] experiences in the various countries, you'll be thrilled to see how the Lord spoke to their home-based intercessors to pray when the battles became fierce. Through their prayers, situations were reversed, language barriers became non-existent, healings and miracles took place as lives were touched by the power of the Holy Spirit.[4]

In 1993, 188 prayer journey teams took 257 prayer journeys into the nations of the 10/40 Window. This figure only includes those from which Christian Information Network received reports. How many others also journeyed but did not report is difficult to say, but some think it might have been an equal number. The teams were equipped this first time by receiving only a minimum of spiritual mapping information—in this case a one-half page miniprofile of the nation prepared by George Otis Jr.'s Sentinel Group. Later on, however, this information was expanded into a four-page profile of each nation, including historical background, unreached peoples, spiritual competition, noteworthy trends and national prayer concerns for each.

The resultant book, *Strongholds of the 10/40 Window,* is one of the most vital information-packed guides available for intercessors. In it, George Otis Jr. mentions the "voracious appetite" intercessors have for information. "People don't just want to pray," Otis says, "they want to pray intelligently. They want to ensure that their prayers will have a genuine impact on the spiritual battle raging over specific communities and people groups. To accomplish this, they understand, requires accurate targeting coordinates."[5]

Some further targeting coordinates for 1995 and 1997 are found in the two books already mentioned, *Praying Through the 100 Gateway Cities of the 10/40 Window* and *The Unreached Peoples.* In October 1995, 233 prayer journey teams made up of 2,465 intercessors from 48 nations took 607 prayer journeys. These are official Christian Information Network figures, but I would not be surprised if as many as 10,000 intercessors actually made prayer journeys, many of which, for a number of reasons, were never reported.

LOVING OUR ENEMIES

When the project was first taking shape, I shared with Paul Ariga, the A.D. 2000 United Prayer Track coordinator for Japan, that four of the Gateway Cities were located in his nation. I also told him that some 400 intercessors would be coming to Japan, 100 to each of the cities, simply to pray God's blessing on the Japanese. Then I challenged him: "If Japan is receiving 400 intercessors in October 1995, how about reciprocating by sending 400 Japanese intercessors to other cities in the 10/40 Window?"

He responded somberly, "No, we're not going to do that!" After giving me a moment to absorb such an unexpected statement, a wide smile came over his face and Ariga said, "We would not send only 400, we will send 800—two Japanese for each one who comes here!"

Sure enough, 800 Japanese intercessors went out to pray. Where did they go? The Japanese chose to take prayer journeys to the 23 Asian cities Japan had invaded in World War II. They repented to the people there for the atrocities their nation had committed against them and beseeched God for rich blessings upon their former enemies!

The plan for Praying Through the Window III is to have at least one prayer journey team pray "on site with insight" on the home turf of each one of the 1,739 most significant unreached people groups. It might well be that during this initiative as many as 16,000 intercessors will travel millions of miles at their own expense. This they will do in the belief that their prayers will make a difference in releasing multitudes from the oppression of the enemy and allowing them the opportunity to come from darkness to light and from the power of ·ʻ Satan to God.

WHAT DIFFERENCE DOES IT MAKE?

The three most formidable anti-Christian blocs in the world are Buddhism, Hinduism and Islam. There are many others, but none more deeply entrenched, better informed and corporately determined to thwart the advance of the kingdom of God. If we are correct in saying that the great prayer movement has truly begun to blossom in the 1990s, we expect that powerful prayer will begin to make a difference. As might be expected, prayer has been making a considerable difference.

As a starter, reports are coming in that a number of the original 1,739 unreached people groups have been reached as of this writing. The Joshua Project 2000 of the A.D. 2000 Movement is in the process of developing systems for verifying such reports, but they are not yet in place. I personally have no doubt that many of these reports will prove to be true, and that they will increase in frequency month by month. Stay tuned!

More specifically, let's look at the three major anti-Christian forces.

Buddhism: "On the Run!"

My current observations lead me to believe that the principalities over Buddhism are "on the run." This may be the first large wall, after Communism, to come down in our generation. For years Buddhism has been taking serious hits in South Korea, and more recently, on a greater scale, in mainland China. China was the brightest new light for the gospel in the 10/40 Window in the 1980s and it continues even brighter today.

The bright new light of the Buddhist world in the 1990s,

however, seems to be Thailand. Two recent trips have convinced me that our prayers are being answered there, and also that Thailand will be a chief instrument in the hands of God for taking the gospel to Laos, Myanmar (Burma), Cambodia and Vietnam.

My first visit to Thailand was with an indigenous Thai network called The Hope of God for a teaching assignment at their annual church camp. I was amazed, in a nation where Christianity has struggled for 150 years, to see 10,000 believers meeting in a beautiful beachside resort hotel for praise, prayer, refreshment, training and inspiration. My friend Joseph C. Wongsak, the founder, reports that at this writing they have 24 weekly services in their huge Bangkok church, 722 churches throughout almost every district of Thailand and 32 Hope of God churches in 16 other nations.

My second ministry assignment in Thailand was to teach at a conference of 3,500 leaders during the day, and crowds of up to 6,000 in the evenings. They were mostly Pentecostals, but leaders from many of the traditional denominations were there as well. The two other featured speakers were T. L. Osborn and David Yonggi Cho, both of whom knew the Thai situation better than I did.

When I questioned them, Osborn said, "I had been preaching the gospel in many nations of the world, some extremely difficult, before I first came to Thailand in 1956. Thailand turned out to be the darkest nation I had visited up to that time, and I have not been in a darker one since. However, something has changed. In 1996 the Spirit of God is clearly flowing freely in this nation."

Cho said, "I have been coming to Thailand regularly for 20 years. Every time I have come, I have felt sick from the pervasive spiritual oppression in this country. This is the first time in memory that I am here feeling total spiritual freedom!"

Several Thai church leaders told me that it is now easy to

lead the Thai to Christ. When I asked them when they had noticed the change, their estimates seemed to revolve around October 1993, perhaps the first month 21 million believers had prayed in one accord on one day for the evangelization of Thailand.

Yes, prayer truly is making a difference!

Hinduism: "Badly Battered!"

The demonic principalities over Hinduism are "badly battered." Nepal, in the Himalaya Mountains, is the only Hindu kingdom in the world, and it has recently become one of the brightest lights for the gospel in the 10/40 Window. Seeds were planted through the years by the social work of the United Mission to Nepal and more recently by the *Jesus* film of Campus Crusade for Christ, by literature distributed by Every Home for Christ and by other ministries.

Many Nepali Christians were willing to serve six-year jail sentences as a penalty for their conversions to Christ. Then in 1990, some technical changes were made in the national constitution to allow a bit more freedom. It is still supposed to be a crime to convert to Christianity, but the law is not being strictly enforced, and churches are multiplying from north to south, from east to west. When I recently visited Nepal to help dedicate a large worship center and Bible school, leaders were estimating that 200,000 to 300,000 people had become Christians in their country. One said that churches were multiplying so rapidly, just in the capital city of Katmandu, that it was impossible to keep count.

The dramatic India earthquake I mentioned earlier was but one indication that India, the largest stronghold of Hinduism, has been battered. Most Christians in India have come from the south, but many reports of breakthroughs and of multiplying churches through signs and wonders are now coming out of northern India. For example, the Himalayan state of Sikkim, previously staunchly resistant to Christianity, has opened substantially since October 1993. Some reports place the number of believers there at 20 percent, even 30 percent in some places.

John DeVries of Mission 21 India visited Calcutta in October 1995. He reports the following:

> I have been to Calcutta many times and every time I go it is a most depressing experience. I get depressed dreading going; the depression is increased being there; and it takes a few weeks afterwards to recover. But it was totally different in October 1995. I landed in the Airport on Monday and was amazed at how clear and sunny and clean it all looked! As I went to my hotel, my emotions were light. I was full of optimism and a sense of victory. I was utterly surprised at the hymns of praise which were arising in my spirit as I traveled the streets of Calcutta, which suddenly and mysteriously that day did not look nearly as dark and dreary as usual.
>
> When I checked in to my hotel, I was informed that there was a prayer team from Calgary, Alberta, on the fourth floor, and then I realized what was happening. It was the month of Praying Through the Window II! Christians from around the world were praying for the Gateway Cities of the 10/40 Window. This was Monday, and on Wednesday my prayer calendar told me that what turned out to be 36 million would be focusing on Calcutta. I had a strange sensation that Kali, the black goddess of destruction and the patron deity of the area, had temporarily vacated the premises and had taken many companion demons with her. The usual dark, dismal, spiritual cloud which hangs over that city as demonic smog had been blown away by the prayers of God's people![6]

Does prayer make a difference in the Hindu strongholds of the 10/40 Window? Ask John DeVries.

Islam: "Deeply Concerned!"

The principalities over Islam are the strongest of the three religions. I cannot say they are "on the run" or "badly battered," but they definitely seem to be "deeply concerned." One development that has shaken them is the embarrassingly large number of Muslims in Indonesia, the world's largest Muslim nation, who are becoming Christians, although conversions are officially frowned upon by the government. For obvious face-saving reasons the government does not make public their religious census.

Praying through Ramadan. The government must also be deeply concerned by the annual 30 days of Muslim prayer focus during the high holy time of fasting in Ramadan, which is observed in January and February at different times each year. This is one of the Muslims' "five pillars of the faith," and they fast from sunrise to sunset for 30 days. A superb 30-day prayer guide is now available to the Muslims, and is updated each year. An attractive version for children is also available. Now that the prayer guide is on the Internet, it is possible that 10 million Christians will be fervently praying for Muslims "in one accord" for 30 days each year.

We instruct our people always to pray blessing on Muslims. We never pray curses. Furthermore, we recommend praying to God that He will answer the Muslims' prayers. This may sound strange at first until we realize that one of the chief prayers of Muslims during their time of fasting is, "God, please reveal yourself to me." We agree with them on that. It cannot be a coincidence that in the decade of the 1990s, more reports of divine visitations to Muslims have been coming in than perhaps in the previous 100 years combined. In areas where it is forbidden to share the gospel in any way, bright lights are shining, angels are appearing, Jesus shows up, healings take place, voices are heard, visions materialize and vivid dreams communicate the gospel message.

PRAYER EXPEDITIONS

As I have said, two of the newer forms of prayer outside of our churches are prayer journeys and prayer expeditions. The prayer journey typically involves a team traveling to a certain predetermined place, praying for a few days or a week, and then returning home.

The prayer expedition requires considerably higher commitment because the team travels, usually by foot, from one determined place to another, opening entire regions to the presence and flow of the Holy Spirit. Prayer expeditions have recently taken place from Berlin to Moscow, from San Diego to San Francisco, and following the path of General Sherman's march during the War Between the States in the South of the United States, to heal wounds inflicted by the North on the South and by the South on the North, just to name a few. Such expeditions require a substantial amount of planning and the highest quality of spiritual mapping if they are going to meet standards and if the prayer action is to be of the powerful kind.

REPENTING FOR THE CRUSADES

Back to Islam. I would not be greatly surprised if the one current prayer initiative that has the principalities over Islam the most frightened is the Reconciliation Walk. I had the privilege of being in Cologne, Germany, on Easter Sunday 1996, the nine-hundredth anniversary of the departure of the First Crusade, led by Peter the Hermit.

Along with Loren Cunningham and Lynn Green, both of YWAM, I helped pray for and commission the first prayer expedition team, setting out to walk all the known routes of the First Crusade through Europe, the Balkans, Turkey and the Middle East and timed to enter Jerusalem in July 1999. An anticipated tens of thousands of Christians will join this expedition for shorter or longer periods of time, coordinated by Lynn Green's office in London, England, having only one agenda item: sincere corporate repentance for the sins committed by our Christian forebears against Muslims and Jews.

On that Easter Sunday afternoon, the prayer team secured permission to enter the mosque in Cologne to read its one-page declaration of repentance to the imam, the Muslim equivalent of a pastor. When they finished, tears were noticeable in the eyes of the imam. "This message is astonishing," he said. "Whoever had this idea must have had an epiphany of God!"

The imam was so moved that he promised to send the message to all 600 mosques in Germany, which he subsequently did. Weeks later a prayer team member stumbled onto a huge open-air gathering of some 3,000 Muslims in Vienna, Austria. She was amazed when she heard the leader say to the crowd, "The Christians are going through Europe repenting of the sins of the Crusades against us Muslims. This is wonderful. Now, I think, it is time that we begin to repent of our sins against the Christians!"

In Turkey, an awesome reception met the prayer teams when they arrived in October 1996. Lynn Green reports·

> From their arrival at the border of Turkey, the team experienced a welcome far beyond their expectations. I had been in Istanbul ten days earlier and had given an interview to the General Secretary of the Press Association. That article was published on the day the team arrived, so they were met by TV cameras, reporters and an official guard of anti-terrorist police to accompany them.[7]

In Istanbul, the Deputy Mufti, the second most powerful Muslim leader in the city, held a personal reception for 25 of the team in his office, welcomed them with warmth and appreciation, and said, "This message is very important for Turkey."

HEALING WOUNDS OF THE PAST

The reason this seems so important to me ties in with what was said about identificational repentance in chapter 5. Muslims have been the most resistant of the major anti-Christian blocs for centuries. In all probability, the major stronghold providing Satan a legal excuse for blinding their minds to the gospel of Christ was erected by the Christian crusaders who, among other things, mercilessly slaughtered 30,000 Muslims and burned alive 6,000 Jews when they entered Jerusalem in 1099. They did all this under the banner of the cross, announcing that they were doing things such as murdering women and children in the name of Jesus! Although many Christians in our churches are unaware of these and some even worse atrocities, Muslims are not. As far as they are concerned, these things are as real as if they had happened last week.

I like the way Kjell Sjöberg of Sweden explains this kind of thing. He says:

> Guilt that has never been dealt with is an open invitation to demonic powers. Before we can bind the strongman, we need to deal with sins that have given the enemy a legal right to occupy. The devil and his principalities have been defeated by Jesus on the cross and they would not be able to stay on unless they were relying on old invitations that have never been canceled.[8]

Sincere repentance, on a scale proportionate to the magnitude of the offense, is a major tool to help neutralize the pow-

erful forces of darkness that have succeeded in keeping follow-
ers of Mohammed captive through the centuries. The Reconciliation Walk could be the very instrument God uses to crack open
the Islamic barriers to the gospel, opening the way for millions
and millions personally to experience the love of God through
Jesus Christ. If this is correct, it is little wonder the demonic powers over Islam are, to say the least, "deeply concerned."

SINGING THE "NEW SONG"

The Holy Spirit is calling God's people everywhere to pray for
the nations. They are responding in exponentially increasing
numbers. The golden bowls are filling fast. It may not be too
long from now that the elders and living creatures are able to
sing the "new song" to the Lamb on the throne: "[You] have
redeemed us to God by Your blood out of every tribe and
tongue and people and nation" (Rev. 5:9).

■ REFLECTION QUESTIONS ■

1. All nations of the world need prayer. Why, then, is so much
   emphasis being given to the nations of the 10/40 Window?
2. What do you think of the idea "the more prayer the better"?
   Is there more power in larger quantities of prayer?
3. Review the reports of spiritual powers over Buddhism, Hinduism and Islam and then comment on them.
4. Discuss the possible effects of the Reconciliation Walk along
   the routes of the First Crusade.

Notes

1. This story of the Wa was reported in the *Jesus Film Project* newsletter 12, no. 3 (March
   1996), and distributed on the Internet by Steve Bufton, Friday Fax 34, September 19,
   1996.
2. Dutch Sheets, *Intercessory Prayer* (Ventura, Calif.: Regal Books, 1996), p. 209.

3. "While They Slept," *Time* (October 11, 1993).
4. Beverly Pegues, ed. "Introduction," *WindoWatchman* (1994): 12.
5. George Otis Jr., ed., *Strongholds of the 10/40 Window: Intercessor's Guide to the World's Least Evangelized Nations* (Seattle: YWAM Publishing, 1995), p. 9.
6. Personal correspondence from John DeVries.
7. Personal letter to C. Peter Wagner from Lynn Green, November 8, 1996.
8. Kjell Sjöberg, "Spiritual Mapping for Prophetic Prayer Actions," *Breaking Strongholds in Your City*, ed. C. Peter Wagner (Ventura, Calif.: Regal Books, 1993), pp. 108-109.

FURTHER RESOURCES

- *Strongholds of the 10/40 Window* edited by George Otis Jr. (Seattle: YWAM Publishing, 1995). This book contains an intercessor's profile of each of the 62 nations of the 10/40 Window. It is essential for targeted prayer for the nations.

- *Intercessory Prayer* by Dutch Sheets (Ventura, Calif.: Regal Books, 1996). This is arguably the top current textbook about aggressive prayer.

- *Life-Changing Encounters* edited by Debra Sanders (Caleb Project, 10 West Dry Creek Circle, Littleton, CO 80120, 1995). This a handbook for those who wish to go on short-term mission trips and help research the unreached people groups. It is full of practical advice.

- *Praying Through the 100 Gateway Cities* edited by C. Peter Wagner, Stephen Peters and Mark Wilson (Seattle: YWAM Publishers, 1995). This book includes profiles and prayer points for each of the Gateway Cities of the 10/40 Window.

- *The Unreached Peoples* edited by Patrick Johnstone, John Hanna and Marti Smith (Seattle: YWAM Publishers, 1996). This book profiles 146 "Gateway Clusters," which include the 1,739 significant yet unreached people groups of the 10/40 Window.

Innovative Praying

T HERE IS HARDLY ANY LIMIT TO THE CREATIVITY BEING released now that the word is spreading across the Body of Christ concerning powerful prayer, spiritual mapping, identificational repentance, prayerwalking, prayer journeys and praying outside of the churches. The sheer delight of entering into prayer efforts, large and small, are accompanied by the faith that God will truly use these entities to make a difference and to bring lost souls into His kingdom. I believe we are seeing more "innovative praying" today than ever before in the history of the Church. This chapter will only be able to scratch the surface and mention but a few interesting cases.

For example, in the United States, every first Thursday of May has been designated as the National Day of Prayer. A National Prayer Committee is chaired by David Bryant of Concerts of Prayer, and Shirley Dobson of Focus on the Family chairs the National Day of Prayer Task Force. Since 1995, a nationally televised concert of prayer has become part of this event, drawing the personal participation of scores of top-ranking Christian leaders, and uniting millions in simultaneous prayer right in their homes and in church groups that meet for that purpose.

A PRAYER INVASION BY LAND, SEA AND AIR

Among the most innovative of prayer leaders is Ed Silvoso of Harvest Evangelism and author of a key book about prayer evangelism, *That None Should Perish* (Regal Books). After a fact-finding tour to meet with pastors of the San Francisco Bay area not too long ago, Silvoso perceived a kind of "spiritual pregnancy" pervaded the region. In almost every city of the area, pastors had begun joining together for prayer. It seemed as if the time was ripe to do something unusual in the entire Bay Area on the National Day of Prayer in 1996. Few cities have ever been prayed for this way.

On May 2, 1996, at 9:00 A.M., four major prayer actions began simultaneously:

1. Airplanes took off from every airport in the area, carrying intercessors who established a mantle of prayer over the metropolitan area.
2. Boats full of pray-ers lifted anchor and sailed throughout all the waters of the Bay, beseeching God for His power.
3. Motorcyclists revved up their engines and prayed all day along the freeway arteries.
4. Intercessors boarded all forms of public transportation from buses to trolleys to ferries to tramways, crisscrossing the entire area with prayer.

A group prayed on the steps of City Hall. Teams that had previously done appropriate spiritual mapping took prayer journeys to key strongholds of darkness, combating spiritual hosts of wickedness over the area.

Meanwhile, believers gathered in nine cities surrounding the Bay Area at 7:14 P.M. (reflecting 2 Chron. 7:14). A group of pastors from each of the cities was commissioned before the Lord by the participants of their own city's prayer meeting. They then boarded a bus and traveled together to the next city, praying for certain places and needs that had been mapped out along the way. They joined together for prayer with the group gathered there. In that way, the pastors—who, as we have discussed, are the spiritual gatekeepers of an area—generated a complete circle of prayer around the Bay Area by each group traveling to the next city. That evening, a local radio station connected all nine cities together for praise, celebration and celebrating the Lord's Supper. What an awesome day of prayer it was for greater San Francisco![1]

But it did not end there. Since then, a new spiritual climate has permeated the Bay Area. In January 1997, more than 240 pastors joined together in a Prayer Summit. Billy Graham agreed to conduct a crusade there, and at this writing believers are moving toward establishing 15,000 "lighthouses of prayer" throughout the region.

PRAYER ON THE RADIO WAVES

In chapter 8 I mentioned the women intercessors of Goiania, Brazil, who were called in by government officials to give direction in handling a serious prison riot. The key to opening the way for such a thing to happen was their daily radio prayer meeting that blanketed the city. It is estimated they now have more than 100,000 in Goiania who pray "in one accord" next to the radios in their homes each Friday for a minimum of two hours.

When we report that 36 million participated in the Praying Through the Window II initiative, interceding for the same cities on the same day for 31 days, an important fact emerges. The largest single bloc of the pray-ers is found in mainland China. These are people in house churches, persecuted for their faith, who have few resources such as books, magazines or Bibles.

These Chinese Christians have found ways, though, of tuning in to Christian radio stations such as the Far Eastern Broadcasting Company, and the majority of them are very faithful listeners. They form habits of listening to the same programs at the same times every single day. All the major international Christian radio ministries are aware of this and are participating in the Praying Through the Window efforts. The radio broadcasters, whose voices are well known to the millions of loyal listeners, lead actual prayer meetings in Mandarin or Cantonese or other Chinese dialects. They follow the prayer calendars, books and other resources being circulated for the purpose of stimulating powerful simultaneous prayer.

Peru entered this decade under a deep cloud of darkness perpetrated by the notorious Shining Path guerrillas. Few other nations have been more tormented by murder, arson, terrorism and anarchy than Peru was in those days. It was powerful enough to put a virtual lid on the activities of the evangelical churches of the nation for a time. Things are totally different now, however, and Peru is enjoying some of the most dynamic evangelism and church growth in all of Latin America.

What brought about the change? I recently visited Peru and sought the answer to that question from Christian leaders. Many pointed to a series of visits by Harold Caballeros, a Guatemalan pastor and the leader of the Hispanic American Spiritual Warfare Network. He began to teach them that strategic-level intercession could push back the oppressive powers of darkness. That was an important key. More leaders, though, mentioned the change was brought about by Radio Pacifico, a Christian radio station that began uniting believers in prayer over the radio waves regularly around 1993. At the time of my visit, 20,000 were regularly praying "in one accord" for their nation and for those in authority. The result? Peru has taken a radical change for the good!

CHILDREN ARE PRAYING

Many are surprised when they first hear that God is raising up large numbers of children, 6 to 14 years of age or so, who are praying on an adult level. This does not seem to be an isolated phenomenon, because consistent reports of this are coming in from many diverse nations of the world.

Biblical Christians will have no problem believing that God would do such a thing. Jesus' words when he cleansed the Temple are well known: "It is written, 'My house shall be called a house of prayer'" (Matt. 21:13). On the same occasion, though, the chief priests and scribes were complaining that *children* were loudly lifting up their voices in praise, saying, "Hosanna to the Son of David!" (v. 15). Jesus responded to them: "Have you never read, 'Out of the mouth of [children]...You have perfected praise'?" (v. 16). There is more.

Jesus was quoting Psalm 8 where it goes on to indicate that the prayers of children have great power in spiritual warfare, saying that what comes out of their mouths will "silence the enemy and the avenger" (Ps. 8:2). Perhaps that is one of the reasons Jesus tells us that unless we "become as little children, [we] will by no means enter the kingdom of heaven" (Matt. 18:3).

The Esther Network International of West Palm Beach, Florida, is taking the lead in mobilizing and networking children from around the world to pray for world evangelization. Linked with the A.D. 2000 United Prayer Track, Esther Ilnisky formed a team of 40 children intercessors from various nations who were enrolled (having the same status as adults) as official delegates to the huge A.D. 2000 Global Consultation on World Evangelization (GCOWE) held in Seoul, Korea, in 1995. The word about powerful children's prayers was made public, and day after day long lines of adults, among them

---

On a certain date every September,... students are joining hands and praying around their school flagpole....[It] does not violate the separation of church and state.

---

some of the most highly respected Christian leaders of the world, were patiently waiting their turn to receive individual prayer ministry from the children. Subsequent reports from GCOWE '95 delegates frequently mentioned how significant the prayers of the children had been in their own lives and ministries. Esther Ilnisky reports that, at this writing, she has established contact with and is networking nearly 2 million praying children.

"See You At The Pole" is an innovative prayer initiative aimed first at middle schools and high schools of the United States, but has since spread to other continents of the world. In 1990, a group of students from a Christian youth group in Burleson, Texas, sensed that the Lord wanted them to go to their school and pray. They obeyed God. At first it seemed to their pastor, Billy Beacham, that it was just another prayer meeting. In the providence of God, however, the news got out and young people across the country began to say, "We want to do what they're doing in Texas." Now the National Network of

Youth Ministries in San Diego, California, helps coordinate what has become a movement.

Because every school has a flagpole in its yard, that became the place to pray. Now on a certain date every September, near the beginning of the school year, students are joining hands and praying around their school flagpole. In 1996, it was estimated that up to 3 million children in the United States from approximately 75 percent of our high schools participated. Responding to the complaints of some staunch opponents of prayer, the Supreme Court declared "See You At The Pole" as a constitutional activity that does not violate the separation of church and state.

FASTING AND PRAYER

Through the years in my Christian experience, I recognized that fasting was biblical and that Christians probably should do it, but it never became much of a part of my personal lifestyle. For one thing, I had no role models. I sensed an unspoken general agreement not to talk about fasting too much, and particularly not to tell anyone else if you did happen to fast. After all, did Jesus not say that when we fast we should do it in a secret place and not let anyone know (see Matt. 6:18)? Because of a wrong application of this Scripture, I believe the prayers of many of us in those days lacked the true power they should have had.

In this remarkable decade of the 1990s, however, fasting has become a hot topic, high on the agendas of Christian leaders across the theological spectrum. The icebreaker was Bill Bright of Campus Crusade, who was led by the Lord to go on a personal 40-day fast early in the decade. Unlike some of his peers, Bright was not reticent to talk about and to recommend serious fasting to the whole Body of Christ.

In December 1994, Bill Bright called together the Christian

leaders of America for nothing but three days of fasting and prayer in Orlando, Florida. Because such a thing had never been done before, he had no idea what the response might be. He gave only a few months' advance notice, and many of the leaders he was inviting typically had calendars filled one to two years in advance. The response, however, was amazing. More than 600 leaders, representing more than 100 denominations came together at their own expense to get down on their knees before the Lord on behalf of their nation and other

> Prayer along *with serious fasting,* if done in one accord and on a massive scale by the people of God in a given nation, can and will release the hand of God to literally transform the whole nation.

nations of the world. Such events, growing in size, have become part of American Christian life for some years now. A 1996 Prayer and Fasting meeting in St. Louis, Missouri, drew an astounding 3,700 who gave up food for three days to pray for revival.

FASTING AND SPIRITUAL AWAKENING

Bright is convinced that "America and much of the world will, before the end of the year 2000, experience a great spiritual awakening. This divine visit of the Holy Spirit from heaven will kindle the greatest spiritual harvest in the history of the Church. But before God comes in revival power, the Holy Spirit will call millions of God's people to repent, fast, and pray in the spirit of 2 Chronicles 7:14."[2] In that Scripture God says, "If My people who are called by My name will humble themselves, and pray and seek My face, and turn from their wicked ways, then I will hear from heaven, and will forgive their sin and heal their land."

Although fasting is not specifically mentioned in that Scripture passage, Bill Bright argues convincingly:

> Fasting is the only discipline that meets all the conditions of 2 Chronicles 7:14. When one fasts, he humbles himself; he has more time to pray, more time to seek God's face, and certainly he would turn from all known sin. One could read the Bible, pray, or witness for Christ without repenting of his sins. But one cannot enter into a genuine fast with a pure heart and pure motive and not meet the conditions of the passage.[3]

Elmer Towns, author of the excellent book *Fasting for Spiritual Breakthrough*, agrees. He says:

> Fasting is not an end in itself; it is a means by which we can worship the Lord and submit ourselves in humility to Him....One of the greatest spiritual benefits of fasting is becoming more attentive to God—becoming more aware of our own inadequacies and His adequacy, our own contingencies and His self-sufficiency—and listening to what He wants us to be and do.[4]

In his book, Towns suggests nine different ways to fast, each one aimed at solving nine different needs in individuals and churches. Each fast follows a different prescription to accomplish its purpose.

Both Bill Bright and Elmer Towns are saying that prayer

along *with serious fasting,* if done in one accord and on a massive scale by the people of God in a given nation, can and will release the hand of God to literally transform the whole nation. Towns says, "If all our churches fasted, they would move forward in evangelism and reach out in feeding and helping others. God would then pour His presence upon His people."[5]

THE WORLD'S LONGEST, RUNNING PRAYER CHAIN

On Easter Sunday 1988, some energetic Youth With a Mission (YWAM) young adults climbed the Mount of Olives, lit an Olympic-style torch, and began running the torch around the world to help stimulate prayer for world evangelization. Since then, thousands have taken part in carrying the prayer torch from city to city and from nation to nation. On one north-south run from Alaska to Antarctica, the team had to change from running shoes to snow boots to complete the route! As of this writing, the "Torch Run," as it is called, has covered 40 countries and logged some 50,000 miles, twice the distance around the earth. Interest continues to build, and the end is nowhere in sight.

The Torch Run may be only one of many causes, but it is a fact that since YWAM began this innovative kind of praying in 1988, prayer for world evangelization in many forms has reached a peak never before seen and it is continuing to soar to new heights every year.

PRAYER QUANTITY: MILLIONS OF HOURS

In these days of the great world prayer movement, prayer has increased in both quantity and quality. Not surprisingly, the Japanese have taken the lead in applying high technology to monitor massive quantities of prayer. Paul Ariga, who heads the A.D. 2000 United Prayer Track in Japan, is also one of the founders of the All Japan Revival Mission. In 1993, they held a massive three-day revival mission in the 60,000-seat baseball stadium of Osaka. In preparation, they decided to enlist what they called "prayer warriors" who would agree to pray regularly for the revival. Along with them they also enlisted a more select group of "fasting prayer warriors" who would promise to combine serious fasting with their prayers.

Each intercessor was required to keep a careful log of the amount of time spent praying for the revival meetings and to record it on a printed card. When 10 hours had been completed, a card was mailed into the office and a new card was begun. A database was set up to keep track of the intercessors and the number of hours they had prayed. Their first goal was 180,000 hours, one hour for each seat in the stadium for the three days, but by the time of the meetings it had been doubled to 350,000 hours of prayer, two hours for each seat. A record 22,000 attendees registered conversions to Christ at the meetings!

The intercessors did not want to stop, though. They were so encouraged by the first results that Paul Ariga and others decided to aim their sights higher and set a goal of 1 million recorded hours of prayer for revival in Japan. In October 1996, they were able to announce they had reached 1,001,104 hours! By then, they had registered 15,175 prayer warriors and 2,896 fasting prayer warriors. They still did not want to stop. Their current prayer plan began by researching the number of square kilometers in Japan—377,750—and aiming for one hour of prayer for each square kilometer before their next revival meeting in Tokyo in 1998. My guess is that they will go far beyond that. They now publish a national toll-free number for new people who desire to enroll as prayer warriors.

PRAYER QUALITY: VIOLENT PRAYER

As I have mentioned several times, the 1990s seems to be the decade, more than any previous one, in which Christians are stepping out in aggressive spiritual warfare. By the power of the Holy Spirit we are now invading the territory of the enemy in overt and unprecedented ways. Warfare, by definition, involves violence. Our violence is not physical, though; it is *spiritual* violence. "For the weapons of our warfare are not carnal but mighty in God for pulling down strongholds" (2 Cor. 10:4).

Because our major weapon of spiritual warfare is prayer, it could be expected that the prayers of the 1990s might be of a more violent quality than much of our previous praying. This is, in fact, happening. For example, the subtitle of Cindy Jacobs's influential book *Possessing the Gates of the Enemy* (Chosen Books) is: *A Training Manual for Militant Intercession.* In the 1980s this kind of a book probably would not have become a best-seller, as it is in the 1990s.

In a recent bulletin of The Church On The Way in Van Nuys, California, Pastor Jack Hayford wrote a column he called "A Time for Holy Violence!" A woman, praying for her city in front of a large group of Los Angeles pastors and leaders, had a week prior to that cried out emotionally, "Be violent! Be violent!"

Hayford reports, "The call was instantly responded to; understood clearly by the large team of spiritual leaders present who knew Jesus' words: 'The kingdom of heaven suffers violence, and the violent take it by force' (Matt. 11:12). It's the central statement in a passage where our Lord declares the principle: There are no slick or smooth ways to break through unto spiritual victory—a holy violence is necessary!"[6]

Urging his congregation to engage in "holy war in the invisible realm," Hayford goes on to say:

There is nothing—again, NOTHING!!—more basic or

essential to victorious prayer than violent prayer. It's prayer that breaks the rules of human reserve; tears that erode our neat composure; strong cries that rise above recitations of religious words. This praying becomes powerful, not because it's vibrant with emotion, but because it has broken the bonds of mere reason alone. It *has* reason, and the words spoken do have a coherence born of the *mind* of God, but the passion that gives them force streams from His *heart!*[7]

This is a highly significant word, not only for Jack Hayford's congregation, but also for the whole Body of Christ.

PROPHETIC PRAYER ACTS

The term "prophetic prayer acts" was new to me when I first heard it not too long ago. As the worldwide prayer movement expands, though, and as the power behind our praying increases tremendously, prophetic prayer acts are becoming more and more common. Often in the prophetic prayer act the violence about which Jack Hayford speaks reaches peaks of intensity.

I include prophetic prayer acts in a chapter about innovative prayer not because prophetic prayer acts are new—the Scripture is full of them. I include them because (1) they are so different from the ways a large number of us who come from the more traditional streams have been used to praying, and (2) innovation and creativity seem to be woven into the very fabric of prophetic prayer acts. However, this does not refer to *human* innovation or creativity. The word "prophetic" is used partly because the design for any given prayer act, if it is authentic, comes through revelation through two-way prayer, as I described in chapter 2. In a word, it is *divine* innovation and creativity.

To get in tune with the concept of prophetic prayer acts,

we need only to flash back to our basic knowledge of the Old Testament. At one point, for example, God told Jeremiah to bury his underwear under a rock on the banks of the Euphrates River. My version does not use the term "underwear," but the *Contemporary English Version* calls them "linen shorts," which needs no further explanation (see Jer. 13:1, *CEV*). After a long time, God sent Jeremiah back to dig them up, and they had rotted and been ruined. The lesson? God said, "In this manner I will ruin the pride of Judah" (v. 9).

Isaiah was told to walk around naked as a prophetic act. God then said, "Just as My servant Isaiah has walked naked and barefoot three years for a sign and a wonder against Egypt and Ethiopia, so shall the king of Assyria lead away the Egyptians...naked and barefoot, with their buttocks uncovered" (Isa. 20:3,4). This would seem strange if it had not come explicitly from God. Ezekiel was instructed to shave off his hair and beard at one point and to burn one-third of the hair, to strike one-third with a sword and to scatter one-third to the wind (see Ezek. 5:1-4). These acts are innovative and creative, to say the least. But, again, it is *God's* innovation and creativity. Our role is simply to hear and to obey.

HEARING AND OBEYING

Steve Hawthorne and Graham Kendrick say: "Prophetic actions are commonplace in Scripture. People of every generation of faith utilized gesture and demonstrative action. God rolled back the Red Sea, but He put a rod in Moses' hand as a bridge to heaven's power."[8] They then remind us of Joshua taking Jericho by marching around the city seven times, and they comment: "The parade was not designed to be a war dance to intimidate enemies or psych up the warriors. The marches, the shouts, the trumpets were in fact demonstrative prayers, enacted statements of faith."[9]

Nehemiah was facing a serious rash of usury among his people. He had made them promise to return goods to their victims that they should never have taken. Then he said, "I shook out the fold of my garment and said, 'So may God shake out each man from his house, and from his property, who does not perform this promise'" (Neh. 5:13).

Kjell Sjöberg, the head of the Spiritual Warfare Network in Sweden, was on a prayer journey to Budapest, Hungary, when God led him to review Nehemiah's prophetic act. They had already discerned that the territorial spirit opposing the kingdom of God was a spirit of slavery. Here is how Sjöberg tells it: "When we came against the spirit of slavery and proclaimed freedom in Budapest, we all stood and shook our jackets and clothes as a prophetic act. May the Lord shake up those who do not release their brothers, just as we are shaking our jackets! We shook them violently under the power of the Holy Spirit."[10] Once again, that word "violence" surfaces.

Dutch Sheets gives us an excellent definition of a prophetic act: "Prophetic action or declaration is something said or done in the natural realm at the direction of God that prepares the way for Him to move in the spiritual realm, which then consequently effects change in the natural realm." He then rephrases it: "God says to do or say something. We obey. Our words or actions impact the heavenly realm, which then impacts the natural realm."[11]

ELISHA'S SALT

The water in Jericho was bad. Elisha had just received the prophetic mantle from Elijah. Undoubtedly the elders of Jericho had certain doubts about whether Elisha could fill the shoes of Elijah. So they came to him with the problem of the bad water. Elisha sensed that the time had arrived for a public prophetic act. He said, "Bring me a new bowl, and put salt in it" (2 Kings

2:20). When they did, Elisha went to the source of the water and threw the salt into it. He said to the elders, "Thus says the Lord: 'I have healed this water; from it there shall be no more death or barrenness'" (v. 21). That is exactly what happened and Jericho's water was fine after that.

Lars-Goran Gustafson of Sweden was living with his family in a large home shared by other Christian families. One morning they turned on the faucet and the water came out dark and had a terrible odor. City officials came to inspect it and condemned the water, shutting off the water main between the well and the house. The families had no idea what to do except to pray and ask God for a solution. That evening two of the residents of the house went to church, and the pastor read 2 Kings 2:19-22. They looked at each other and were amazed to find that each of them, independent of the other, had read exactly the same passage in their devotions that very morning. They concluded they must be hearing from God.

So they gathered the group living in the house, read the 2 Kings Scripture and then asked themselves if they had enough nerve to try to do what Elisha did. It was not easy because this was back in the 1980s when few people were talking about bold prayers and prophetic acts. They prayed and asked each other if they could have faith equal to that of Elisha. One of them said, "Faith is to act on the Word of God and do what it says. So let's go over the passage again. First, the prophet asked for a new bowl."[12]

It so happened that one of the women had just received a gift of two new bowls, so they put salt in one of them, formed a circle around the well house in the backyard, prayed and threw the salt into the well. When they went back to the house, the water came out of the faucet crystal clear. After four days of testing, the puzzled city officials presented a document to them, which said they now had the best water in the community!

THIRTY SACKS OF RICE

Ravikumar Kurapati, an Indian evangelist, was in trouble. He had gone to a village to plant a new church and one of his first converts was a Hindu farmer. As the season's rice crop grew, the new believer's rice turned out to be the worst in town, full of weeds and wilting plants. He was becoming the butt of jokes and at one point he wondered whether he should have given his life to Jesus. He went to his pastor for prayer. Kurapati encouraged him through the Word of God.

By the next morning, Kurapati had heard from God. He says, "The next day I went with him to his field where almost all the villagers were watching me. I took a bucket of fresh water and prayed. Then I asked the farmer to sprinkle it over his crops."[13] When harvest time came, the amazed farmer reaped no fewer than 30 bags of rice from his field, much more than a plot that size should ever have produced in the best of conditions. The villagers' lives were then opened to the gospel, and a strong church has since been planted.

This is not magic. Salt in water or water over rice crops has no intrinsic power. Prophetic acts do not coerce God to do something we decide He should do. An authentic prophetic act is not the seed for developing a new formula. Steve Hawthorne and Graham Kendrick say, "Recipes for vaporizing evil too easily become magic formulas devoid of the power of the person of Jesus. Satan is always as ready to enchant us with our supposed power as we are to believe that our actions coerce the very heavens into compliance. A good rule of thumb is to assume that most prophetic actions are intended for one time use."[14] This is good advice.

HEAVENLY SEEDS IN A BULGARIAN PARK

Dick Eastman of Every Home for Christ knew about and was

practicing innovative forms of prayer long before many of us could spell "prophetic acts," so to speak. Back in the days before the fall of the iron curtain, he had taken a prayer journey team to Sofia, Bulgaria. Bulgaria's ruthless dictator, Todor Zhivkov, had been in power longer than any Communist dictator since Stalin. As several prayer groups, mostly youth, began to prayerwalk Sofia's central park, Wes Wilson, now a vice president of Every Home for Christ, sensed that he heard the Lord telling him to take his group to a certain clearing to do a prophetic act.

The more they prayed, the bolder they became. Wes led each person in his group to dig a small hole in the dirt as if preparing to plant a seed. Then they all reached up toward heaven as if they were grasping a heavenly seed, and they symbolically planted the invisible seeds into the ground. By that time the Holy Spirit had come among them powerfully and many were weeping. They concluded by spending time praising God. Emboldened beyond his usual demeanor, Wes prophesied aloud: "Someday I believe a revolution overthrowing Communism will come to Bulgaria, and I believe it will begin right here on this very spot." He then added: "I also believe that someday I'll read the answer to this prayer on the front page of the *Los Angeles Times!*"[15]

Sure enough. More than a year later the November 13, 1989, issue of the *Los Angeles Times* carried the headline, "Bulgarians Greet Change With Caution, Suspicion." The story told how the revolution in Bulgaria had begun when a table was set up in a clearing in Sofia's central park so that opponents of the government could sign a petition. Dick Eastman comments: "The initial group of signers was no more than the size of our team of intercessors. But that number would soon grow into hundreds and then thousands. The Bulgarian Revolution had begun! And, as the article explained, it all started in a clearing in Sofia's central park. I think some of our youthful intercessors might recognize that clearing!"[16]

WHAT REALLY CHANGED NEPAL?

In the last chapter, I described the radical changes that have come over the spiritual atmosphere of the Himalayan Hindu kingdom of Nepal in the 1990s. It takes considerable faith to believe that the gospel will be preached to every nation by the end of the year 2000, but recent events in Nepal are incredible faith builders. If it can happen there, it can happen virtually anywhere.

What really changed Nepal? The groundwork for the changes was laid in previous years, when Nepal was a tightly closed nation and where only the bravest of the missionaries would venture. The social workers of the United Mission to Nepal created positive attitudes toward Christians, although they were not allowed to share the gospel. The Bible translators paid a price to bring the Word of God into Nepal. Early converts were willing to risk imprisonment or their lives for the gospel. Although not on today's massive scale, believers in many other parts of the world were praying fervently for a breakthrough in Nepal.

One person who had prayed several days a week for Nepal for many years was Roger Mitchell of Great Britain, the head of the Spiritual Warfare Network for Northern Europe. He had come to faith in Christ as a 16-year-old through Isaiah 55:6: "Seek the Lord while He may be found, call upon Him while He is near."

Roger's conversion was of the more radical, life-changing kind, and in the early days of his new faith, Isaiah 55 would naturally be a focal point for seeking the Lord's direction through the Scriptures. Therefore, Roger read: "For you shall go out with joy, and be led out with peace; the mountains and the hills shall break forth into singing before you" (v. 12). God impressed him so strongly and so personally through these words that Roger acquired an atlas to find out where the highest mountains in the world were located. When he found they were the Himalaya Mountains in Nepal, he was ready to dedicate his life as a missionary to Nepal.

Nepal was closed to missionaries in those days, therefore the actual missionary call never materialized. Since that time, however, Roger Mitchell never faltered as a constant prayer warrior for Nepal. By 1990, he had become a full-time leader in the dynamic Icthus apostolic network led by Roger Forster. Once a year, Icthus planned a large international conference in which they sought God, prayed and strategized their worldwide outreach. Icthus is one of those groups that understood spiritual mapping, strategic-level spiritual warfare, violent prayer and prophetic acts for years before it caught on in the rest of the Body of Christ. Therefore, doing a prophetic act in their annual international conference was nothing out of the ordinary.

"Fall from the Chair When the Stronghold Is Broken!"

At one point, God moved the Icthus group to tape a map of Nepal onto the floor. One of the Nepali friends of Icthus had recently been imprisoned for his faith, and that had prompted the special prayer concentration on Nepal. As a prophetic act, they placed a chair on the map, and Roger, recognized as carrying an extraordinary burden for Nepal, was asked to stand on the chair. The kind of violent intercession Jack Hayford advocates then began in earnest. After a time of fervent prayer, one of the prophetic intercessors said, "Roger, you are now representing the demonic stronghold of darkness over Nepal. We are going to call on the Lord to break that stronghold that has been there for centuries. When it is broken we will know it, and you will then fall off the chair."

They began to pray more aggressively than before. The Lord instructed one of them to read Isaiah 49:7: "The Redeemer of Israel, their Holy One, to Him whom man despises, to Him whom the nation abhors, to the Servant of rulers: 'Kings shall see and arise, princes shall also worship.'"

The "princes" were taken by the group to signify the territorial spirits that had maintained Nepal in spiritual captivity. The intercessors took authority over them in the name of Jesus Christ and through His blood shed on the cross, telling them they were no longer going to rule over Nepal. The release by the Holy Spirit eventually came, and Roger Mitchell fell from the chair to the floor and laid there as if dead for a time. The prophetic act had been completed as God had indicated.

That very weekend, the newspapers carried the headlines that the king of Nepal had agreed to change the constitution, allow more freedom for the Christians and release those who had been imprisoned for their faith in Christ! Nepal has never been the same since. As I mentioned before, reports at this writing reveal that 3,000 Christian churches have been planted in Nepal, at least an equal number of Every Home for Christ "Christ Groups" have started, and possibly 300,000 people are believers. Nepal is now beginning to send missionaries to the equally closed neighboring nations of Bhutan and Tibet.

Was it a mere coincidence that the Icthus group did a prophetic act just days before the change was announced in the media? Skeptics may say yes. Those who understand the power prayer can have on the invisible world, however, will agree that it was no coincidence. Prayers in England played a part in pushing back the territorial spirits over Nepal.

The Last Drop in the Bowl

Remember the golden bowls of Revelation 5? No Icthus leader would ever claim that their prayers were the only ones that filled the bowl representing Nepal. They know, and we know, that God had also been leading untold numbers of other believers on virtually every continent to pray fervently for Nepal, and the incense of their prayers through the years kept filling and filling and filling the bowl. It also could well be that the prophetic act in England provided the final drops that then completely filled the Nepal bowl. If so, this is the point, as Dutch Sheets would say, when God knows that enough prayer has accumulated to get the job done. Then, "He releases power. He takes the bowl and mixes it with fire from the altar" [Rev. 8:5].[17]

God's fire opened Nepal for a massive advance of the kingdom of God. That will continue to happen more and more as God's people grow in their understanding and application of the meaning of the title of this book: *Praying with Power*!

■ REFLECTION QUESTIONS ■

1. Have you personally noticed any special prayer activity among children? Have you heard reports from others?
2. Fasting seems to be more popular among Christians than it has been in the past. What difference do you think this will make?
3. Prophetic prayer acts, whether in Bible days or today, can seem strange. Why would people do such odd things?
4. Which chapter in this book was most meaningful to you? Explain why.

Notes

1. This information was taken from a newsletter from Ed Silvoso dated April 15, 1996, and from a mailing by Bill and Pam Malone of Pray USA! dated April 15, 1996.
2. Bill Bright, *The Coming Revival: America's Call to Fast, Pray, and "Seek God's Face"* (Orlando, Fla.: New*Life* Publications, 1995), p. 29.
3. Ibid., p. 17.
4. Elmer L. Towns, *Fasting for Spiritual Breakthrough* (Ventura, Calif.: Regal Books, 1996), pp. 17-18.
5. Ibid., p. 15.
6. Jack Hayford, "A Time for Holy Violence!" in the bulletin of Church On The Way, Van Nuys, California, March 3, 1996.
7. Ibid.
8. Steve Hawthorne and Graham Kendrick, *Prayerwalking: Praying On-Site with Insight* (Orlando, Fla.: Creation House, 1993), p. 64.
9. Ibid.

10. Kjell Sjöberg, *Winning the Prayer War* (Chichester, England: New Wine Press, 1991), pp. 68-69.
11. Dutch Sheets, *Intercessory Prayer* (Ventura, Calif.: Regal Books, 1996), p. 220.
12. Lars-Goran Gustafson, "Not a Drop to Drink," *Christian Life* (December 1983): 109.
13. From *Dawn Report* (October 1996): 9.
14. Hawthorne and Kendrick, *Prayerwalking*, p. 65.
15. Dick Eastman, *The Jericho Hour* (Orlando, Fla.: Creation House, 1994), p. 19.
16. Ibid., p. 20.
17. Sheets, *Intercessory Prayer*, p. 209.

FURTHER RESOURCES

- *Stories from the Front Lines* by Jane Rumph (Grand Rapids: Chosen Books, 1996). This is the best compilation of dramatic answers to prayer from around the world that we have available.

- The two books I recommend the most about fasting are *The Coming Revival: America's Call to Fast, Pray, and "Seek God's Face"* by Bill Bright (Orlando, Fla.: New*Life* Publications, 1995) and *Fasting for Spiritual Breakthrough: A Guide to Nine Biblical Fasts* by Elmer L. Towns (Ventura, Calif.: Regal Books, 1996).

- *Winning the Prayer War* by Kjell Sjöberg (Chichester, England: New Wine Press, 1991). For those who wish more information about prophetic acts, this is one of the best.

- *Intercessory Prayer* by Dutch Sheets (Ventura, Calif.: Regal Books, 1996). For more about prophetic acts, see the chapter "Actions That Speak and Words That Perform."

- *The Jericho Hour* by Dick Eastman (Orlando, Fla.: Creation House, 1994). This book recounts many creative and innovative prayer actions and reports their dramatic results.

The Prayer Warrior Series Cumulative Index

Using this index, you can trace words, concepts, personalities and Scripture references throughout all six volumes of *The Prayer Warrior Series*. The bold numbers signify the following books:

1—**Warfare Prayer**

2—**Prayer Shield**

3—**Breaking Strongholds in Your City**

4—**Churches That Pray**

5—**Confronting the Powers**

6—**Praying with Power**

For the convenience of those using this as an index for this book, volume 6, *Praying with Power*, all the references are in bold type.

Learn to Fight On Your Knees

THE PRAYER WARRIOR SERIES
from C. Peter Wagner

Warfare Prayer
A biblical and factual guide that will help erase your fears and doubts, leading you to new levels of prayer.
Paperback ISBN 08307.15134 • $10.99
Video SPCN 85116.00612 • $29.99

Prayer Shield
A powerful tool to help organize and mobilize intercessors in the church, providing a defense for the pastor against satanic attacks.
Paperback ISBN 08307.15142 • $10.99
Video SPCN 85116.00620 • $29.99

Breaking Strongholds In Your City
Identify the enemy's territory in your city, focus your prayers and take back your neighborhoods for God.
Paperback ISBN 08307.16386 • $10.99
Video SPCN 85116.00647 • $29.99

Churches That Pray
Examine what prayer is, how prayer builds the local church and how prayer can break down the walls between the church and the community.
Paperback ISBN 08307.16580 • $10.99
Video SPCN 85116.00639 • $29.99

Confronting the Powers
Learn how Jesus and the early church practiced spiritual warfare and what we can learn from their example.
Hardcover ISBN 08307.18192 • $16.99

The Prayer & Spiritual Warfare Video Series
Each tape in this powerful video seminar series features teachings from two respected leaders in the growing prayer movement as they reveal God's vision for today's Church.

Volume 1
Harold Caballeros
Spiritual Warfare
John Eckhardt
Deliverance: Our Spiritual Weapon
Video • UPC 607135.002499 • $19.99

Volume 2
John Dawson
Breaking Strongholds Through Reconciliation
Alice Smith
Intimacy with God
Video • UPC 607135.002536 • $19.99

Volume 3
Cindy Jacobs
Prophetic Intercession
Ted Haggard
Intercessors in the Church
Video • UPC 607135.002505 • $19.99

Volume 4
Jack Deere
The Conspiracy Against the Supernatural
Ed Silvoso
Prayer Evangelism
Video • UPC 607135.001935 • $19.99

Volume 5
Francis Frangipane
Soldiers of the Cross
Ed Silvoso
Doing Greater Works Than Jesus
Video • UPC 607135.002512 • $19.99

Volume 6
James Marocco
Binding and Loosing
Eddie Smith
The Basics of Deliverance
Video • UPC 607135.002529 • $19.99

Loving Your City Into the Kingdom
Ted Haggard and Jack Hayford
Practical, city-reaching strategies for a 21st century revival. Ground-breaking articles from Christian leaders who are witnessing an amazing outpouring of God's love on their communities. Also available as a video seminar featuring Ted Haggard.
Hardcover ISBN 08307.18737 • $17.99
Video (Haggard) UPC 607135-001119 • $39.99

That None Should Perish
Ed Silvoso
Learn the powerful principles of "prayer evangelism" and how you can join with others to bring the gospel to your community.
Paperback ISBN 08307.16904 • $10.99

The Voice of God
Cindy Jacobs
God still speaks to His Church today. This book cuts through the confusion to show how the gift of prophecy can and should be used to edify contemporary churches.
Paperback ISBN 08307.17730 • $10.99
Video UPC 607135-001195 • $39.99
(Available May '97)

Intercessory Prayer
Dutch Sheets
Discover how your prayers can move heaven and earth. Learn the biblical dynamics of intercession and invigorate your prayer life.
Hardcover ISBN 08307.18885 • $16.99

Available at your local Christian Bookstore

Resources for Cutting Edge Leaders

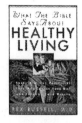

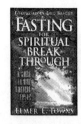

Setting Your Church Free

Neil T. Anderson and Charles Mylander

Spiritual battles can affect entire churches as well as individuals. *Setting Your Church Free* shows pastors and church leaders how they can apply the powerful principles from *Victory Over the Darkness* to lead their churches to freedom.

Hardcover • ISBN 08307.16556

What the Bible Says About Healthy Living

Rex Russell, M.D.

Learn three biblical principles that will help you improve your physical—and spiritual—health. This book gives you practical, workable steps to improve your health and overall quality of life.

Paperback • ISBN 08307.18583

The Healthy Church

C. Peter Wagner

When striving for health and growth of a church, we often overlook things that are killing us. If we can detect and counteract these diseases we can grow a healthy, Christ-directed church.

Hardcover • ISBN 08307.18346

Fasting for Spiritual Breakthrough

Elmer L. Towns

This book gives you the biblical reasons for fasting, and introduces you to nine biblical fasts—each designed for a specific physical and spiritual outcome.

Paperback • ISBN 08307.18397

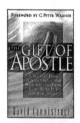

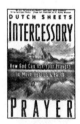

The Voice of God

Cindy Jacobs

Cut through confusion and see how prophecy can be used in any church. You'll get a clear picture of biblical prophecy and how an individual can exercise this spiritual gift to edify the church.

Paperback • ISBN 08307.17730

The Gift of Apostle

David Cannistraci

Find out why God has given the Church apostles—leaders with a clear mission to mobilize and unify the church—and see what the Bible says about the apostolic gift for today's church.

Hardcover • ISBN 08307.18451

Intercessory Prayer

Dutch Sheets

Find inspiration to reach new levels of prayer, the courage to pray for the "impossible" and the persistence to see your prayers through to completion.

"Of all the books on prayer I have read, none compares to Intercessory Prayer!" –C. Peter Wagner

Hardcover • ISBN 08307.18885

That None Should Perish

Ed Silvoso

Ed Silvoso shows that dramatic things happen when we pray for people. Learn the powerful principles of "prayer evangelism" and how to bring the gospel to your community, reaching your entire city for Christ.

Paperback • ISBN 08307.16904

Ask for these resources at your local Christian bookstore.

Regal
A Division of Gospel Light